Marcel Wanders: Pinned Up

25 Years of Design

Ingeborg de Roode

With contributions by:
Marjan Groot
Jennifer Hudson
Penny Sparke
Pietje Tegenbosch
Robert Thiemann and Alexandra Onderwater

Contents

4	**Acknowledgements**
6	**Preface. A Wealth of Contrasts** Karin van Gilst
8	**Introduction. Marcel Wanders in the Stedelijk** Ingeborg de Roode
12	**'Here to Make Our Most Exciting Dreams Come True'** **Marcel Wanders – the Product Designer and Communicator** Ingeborg de Roode
32	**Decoration, Imagination, Seduction. The Work of Marcel Wanders Through Narratives on Ornament and Taste** Marjan Groot
38	**'A Completely Different Animal'** **Interior Design by Marcel Wanders** Jennifer Hudson
50	**Marcel Wanders' Interiors in Context** Penny Sparke
56	**'I'm Interested in You'. An Interview with Marcel Wanders** Robert Thiemann and Alexandra Onderwater

Contents

65   **Marcel Wanders' Most Important Designs – a Selection**
Ingeborg de Roode

     118   **The Knotted Chair**
Ingeborg de Roode

     162   **The Carbon Balloon Chair Held up to the Light**
Ingeborg de Roode

     184   **Marcel Wanders Has a Dream**
Pietje Tegenbosch

193   **Oeuvre 1985–2013**
Ingeborg de Roode in collaboration with Roos Hollander
(Marcel Wanders Studio)

210   **Resumé**

214   **Bibliography**

220   **Index**

223   **About the Authors**

224   **Colophon**

Acknowledgments

'Marcel Wanders: Pinned Up at the Stedelijk. 25 Years of Design,' traces the artistic development of Marcel Wanders. In addition to teams of the Stedelijk Museum and Marcel Wanders Studio, who have deployed their extensive skills to realise this ambitious project, many others have generously contributed their advice and support to make this exhibition possible. We would also like to thank the authors of this publication for their insightful contributions.

The Stedelijk Museum and the artist would like to extend thanks to the following lenders, organisations and persons, without whose support this exhibition and publication would not have been possible. We are grateful to them for their collective generosity and graciousness in helping us bring about this project.

Benefactors
Ahold

Gemeente Amsterdam
Rabobank
Bankgiroloterij

Lenders to the exhibition
Alessi, Crusinallo di Omegna (IT)
B&B Italia, Novedrate (IT)
Baccarat, Paris (FR)
Annette Maria Bakx
Bisazza, Alte (IT)
Boffi, Lentate sul Seveso (IT)
Bonomi, Lumezzane S.S. (IT)
Cappellini, Meda (IT)
Cosme Decorte, Tokyo (JP)
Droog, Amsterdam (NL)
Essenza Home, Amerongen (NL)
Fabbricca Pelleterie Milano, Milaan (IT)
Flos, Bovezzo (IT)
Friedman Benda, New York (US)
Geesa, Amersfoort (NL)
Goods, Amsterdam (NL)
Ton Haas
Holland Electro, Zwolle (NL)
Innovaders, Amsterdam (NL)
Kartell, Noviglio (IT)

Acknowledgments

KDDI, Tokyo (JP)
Keramiekmuseum Princessehof, Leeuwarden (NL)
KLM Royal Dutch Airlines, Schiphol (NL)
Koninklijke Tichelaar Makkum, Makkum, (NL)
KOSE Corporation, Tokyo (JP)
Magis, Torre di Mosto (IT)
Marcel Wanders Studio, Amsterdam (NL)
Moooi, Breda (NL)
Moroso, Cavalicco (IT)
Nationaal Glasmuseum, Leerdam (NL)
NextArt Galéria, Budapest (HU)
Randstad, Diemen (NL)
Senso, Rhenen (NL)
Slide, Buccinasco (IT)
Stedelijk Museum 's-Hertogenbosch, 's-Hertogenbosch (NL)
Stonehage, London (GB)
TextielMuseum, Tilburg (NL)

A Wealth of Contrasts

Karin van Gilst
Managing Director

Handcrafted yet industrial, traditionally knotted yet using a highly advanced material, soft yet hard at the same time. This is a description of the *Knotted Chair* by Marcel Wanders – a description that can likewise be applied to his entire oeuvre, which unites a wealth of contrasts. In 1996, during the annual Salone del Mobile in Milan, Marcel Wanders created a furor with his *Knotted Chair*, the design that marked his international breakthrough. In that same year, the Stedelijk Museum purchased prototype no. 5 of the chair. Now, some 20 years later, Wanders has evolved into one of the Netherlands' most important contemporary designers, and a leading figure on the international design scene.

'Marcel Wanders: Pinned Up. 25 Years of Design' is a large-scale, ambitious exhibition that explores this rich oeuvre. It is the first museum survey of designs produced by Wanders since 1999, and the first major design exhibition following the reopening of the Stedelijk Museum in September 2012. The museum is delighted to present one of the most influential Dutch designers of the last decades.

The Stedelijk has a long tradition of collecting design, reaching back to 1934, when the museum began its collection of applied art and graphic and industrial design. Today, with over 60,000 design objects, the Stedelijk has one of the largest design collections in the Netherlands. The furniture collection occupies a particularly important place in the museum's holdings, with revolutionary designs by Michael Thonet, Marcel Breuer, Gerrit Rietveld, Mart Stam, Verner Panton, and Patrick Jouin. Innovation plays a prominent role in each of these designs. The Stedelijk closely follows new currents and trends in design, and regularly enriches its collection with the work of young designers.

Preface — Karin van Gilst

'Marcel Wanders: Pinned Up' is the result of extensive research and years of preparation by Ingeborg de Roode, the Stedelijk's curator of Industrial Design, in close collaboration with Marcel Wanders and his studio. Their dedication and expertise laid the foundations of this survey exhibition, for which we are very grateful. The extraordinary presentation was designed by Marcel Wanders who – in typical Wanders style – not only created an environment but, more importantly, an experience for the viewer. I am grateful to Marcel Wanders and the people of this studio, in particular Roos Hollander, Sasha Naod, Anna Alberdingk Thijm, Karin Krautgartner, Charlotte Vlerick, Gabriele Chiave and Robin Bevers) for the pleasant and close collaboration that laid the basis for this project.

Without the kind cooperation of the many manufacturers of Wanders' designs, museums, and a number of private individuals who generously supported this presentation by loaning work, mounting a survey of such breadth and depth would have been impossible. I am deeply grateful for their commitment and support.

This publication offers far more than an overview of the exhibition: the essays by Ingeborg de Roode, Marjan Groot, Penny Sparke, Jennifer Hudson, and Pietje Tegenbosch provide an analysis of and context for Wanders' designs. The interview with Wanders by Robert Thiemann and Alexandra Onderwater reveals Wanders' principal drives and motivations. And, thanks to the exhaustive oeuvre list and extensive resumé and bibliography, the publication has become a reference book for 25 years of Wanders designs. My thanks go to Rudolf van Wezel, Robert Thiemann, and Barbara Iwanicka of Frame Publishers for their enthusiasm, professionalism, and fruitful collaboration. I wish to personally thank the following for their valuable contributions: exhibitions project leader Lucas Bonekamp, publications editor Sophie Tates, and project assistant Menno Dudok van Heel.

Finally, my sincere thanks go to all those who helped bring this project to fruition. I am especially grateful to the Municipality of Amsterdam, the Stedelijk Museum Supervisory Board, the Stedelijk Museum founders, and its principal donors and sponsors. And, of course, I wish to express my gratitude to the exhibition sponsor Ahold, whose magnanimous support made this presentation possible.

'Design is a tool that allows us to reach out and inspire, to touch others and help make lives magic and wonderful.'

Marcel Wanders

Marcel Wanders in the Stedelijk

Ingeborg de Roode

Marcel Wanders (Boxtel, 1963) is one of today's most prominent and creative designers. The power of his work lies primarily in how he combines a strong concept or story with remarkable (innovative or handcrafted) materials and techniques, while his visual language often echoes familiar paradigms. The relationship between these elements in his work varies, and from it, a rich and diverse oeuvre has emerged.

Above all, Wanders is a gifted and impassioned communicator. He is an enthusiastic and tireless storyteller who weaves a web of meanings and upbeat connotations into and about his work, sharing them with his audience in a myriad of ways. Wanders deliberately chooses to place the user at the heart of his design process rather than emphasizing developments in the profession, or innovation, or the views of critics. In his introduction to the publication *Interiors*, Robert Thiemann rightly observed that Wanders is more a 'people's designer' than a 'designer's designer'.[1] Isn't that what all designers should be? In industrial and interior design, the chief concern is to create a better environment. We can debate the precise meaning of 'better' long and hard: more aesthetically pleasing, more eco-friendly, more individual, more open. However you look at it, the opinion of the user carries enormous weight. After all, what point is there in an environment that only designers and a handful of others judge to be better?

Since the mid-1990s, Wanders has encapsulated his mission as 'Here to create an environment of love, live with passion, and make our most exciting dreams come true'. In that sense 'our dreams' are those of Wanders but also of others, such as users. Rather than giving people what they want, he gives them what they unknowingly dream of.

In museum circles, Wanders is described as 'creative, innovative and a very inspiring thinker' (Paola Antonelli, MoMA New York), an 'extraordinary design talent' (Gareth Williams, Victoria and Albert Museum), and as 'one of the most influential designers of the 21st century' (R. Craig Miller, Indianapolis Museum of Art).[2]

And museums are not alone in holding the designer in high regard; after all, Wanders is not only one of the most distinguished designers, he is also one of the most successful members of the international design world. In the media, his name has appeared on all manner of prestigious lists for some time, and a plethora of epithets have been used to describe him. In *BusinessWeek* (2002) he was named one of the '25 Leaders of Change' in Europe; in *Elle Decoration* he

[1] R. Thiemann, 'Staging Spaces', in: M. Wanders, et al., *Marcel Wanders. Interiors*, New York 2011, 5.

[2] Paola Antonelli in J. Dalton, 'Boy Wanders', *Financial Times*, 12 April 2003; G. Williams, 'Working Wanders', *Design Week*, 1 February 2002, 17; R. Craig Miller in: R. Craig Miller, P. Sparke, and C. McDermott, *European Design Since 1985. Shaping the New Century*, London/New York 2008, 39.

3 'Wanders. Product Designer, Moooi', *BusinessWeek*, 17 June 2002, 56; 'Designer of the Year', *Elle Decoration* (July 2006), 45; *Identity* [The UAE interior/design/property magazine] (2007) 50, 108; 'a constant font of ideas and energy who is nearly impossible to ignore', J. Scelfo, 'Marcel Wanders on Designing Upbeat Tableware', *The New York Times*, 16 March 2011.

4 Dalton 2003, op. cit. (note 2).

5 Telephone interview between the author and the owner of Alessi, 29 July 2013.

6 J. Veldkamp, 'Dutch Design staat stil', *Elsevier* (2003) oktober, Thema Interieur, 66. 'Communicatively' mentioned in an email by Wanders to the author, 6 December 2013.

7 A. Leclaire, 'Marcel Wanders. Meer is meer', *Vrij Nederland* (2013) 15, 69.

was voted 'Designer of the Year 2005'; in 2007, the magazine *Identity* picked him as one of the 'World's 50 Design Icons', and a few years ago the *New York Times* called him 'the Lady Gaga of design' for his endless flow of ideas and projects.[3] In 2003, Wanders' *Big Shadow* lamp was already one of Italian furniture label Cappellini's bestsellers.[4] Alberto Alessi is also on record as saying that Wanders' designs are among his company's greatest successes.[5]

In the Dutch design world, commercial success tends to be viewed with mistrust. In this regard, Wanders once commented: 'Thinking commercially [or communicatively as he now calls it] is considered taboo. That attitude has to change.'[6] In international circles, Wanders' flair for developing his innovative designs into products and finding a large audience for them is particularly praised. Guus Beumer, director of the Netherlands' design organisation The New Institute which, among other things, supports the development of design in the Netherlands, also commends Wanders for pulling off a 'brilliant feat' and 'being perhaps the only designer truly able to capitalise on the 1990s hype surrounding Dutch Design'.[7] Wanders achieves this by optimising his talent for entrepreneurship (as owner of a large design office and co-owner of several companies) and for communication (through his website, newsletters, art direction for publicity photos, his media performance, and so on).

Few designers possess such a comparable synthesis of creative, business, and communication talent. Philippe Starck, always a role model for Wanders, is one such person. From the 1980s onwards, the French designer has generated prodigious interest in (the design of) products and interiors, whereby he hugely popularised 'design', and made a vital contribution to shaping our environment. Wanders reaps the benefits from this state of affairs. While Starck has since decided to forego product design, yet continues to design, Wanders is at the zenith of his career.

After a 25-year-long career in design, the time has come for a museum to examine Wanders' work. The designer is, as it were, 'pinned up', and his work is subjected to scrutiny. Where better to do this than at the Stedelijk Museum? This museum was among the first to acquire the *Knotted Chair* for its collection, and exhibiting design is one of the Stedelijk's core activities. The exhibition that is accompanied by this publication features a 'white zone' that offers an examination of

Wanders' designs for products and interiors based on ten themes. There is also a 'black zone', where Wanders has created an associative, theatrical installation that emphasises work of a more personal, experimental nature. While this may suggest black-and-white thinking, the presentation reveals to us the subtleties of the designer's vision. A presentation of Wanders' work as art director for his own company Moooi, and for the publicity photos of other brands, is displayed in another separate space. This publication explores all of these areas and themes.

The first essay (pp. 12-31) deals with Wanders' development as a product designer and the analysis of his work focusing on ten themes. Marjan Groot takes this further in her essay that considers such aspects as the use of decoration. In her article, Jennifer Hudson analyses Wanders' interiors, and Penny Sparke places these in an historical-theoretical perspective. In an interview with Robert Thiemann and Alexandra Onderwater, Wanders talks about his process, his ideals, and his position in the design world. The publication is richly illustrated with a selection of Wanders' most important and most visionary designs, ranging from industrial projects to personal work, such as his series of previously unseen digital videos, *Virtual Interiors*. Pietje Tegenbosch wrote a brief analysis of this new series. *The Knotted Chair*, Wanders' best-known design, and the *Carbon Balloon Chair*, an innovative and very recent design, provide material for a case study. Finally, the appendix lists all of Wanders' projects that have made it at least to the serious design stage since 1985, as well as a resumé and a bibliography.

With this exhibition and publication, the Stedelijk Museum adopts a standpoint in the debates about design. One of the central issues in this critical discourse is the extent to which high-quality designs reach a broad public as well as contribute to and enhance our immediate environment.

'Here to Make Our Most Exciting Dreams Come True'

Marcel Wanders – the Product Designer and Communicator

Ingeborg de Roode

Almost all the themes we can identify in Marcel Wanders' work (such as the quest for a more beautiful and better world, building a relationship between user and product, the search for sustainability and use of archetypes) are expressed early on in his career, through interviews, writings and in the work itself. His ideals remain remarkably constant. Yet this by no means implies that Wanders has not since developed his vision, or broadened his work sphere. Quite the contrary; the designer has created a body of work that ranges from jewellery, furniture and consumer products, to interior design, architecture studies and autonomous objects. And, over time, the sensibility of Wanders' work has also undergone profound changes. In this article, both Wanders' developments and constants – particularly in relation to product design – will be discussed.

Fig. 1 **Ettore Sottsass, *Ashoka*, floor lamp, 1981, Memphis, Milaan, metal lacquered and chrome-plated brass and steel, collection Stedelijk Museum Amsterdam.**

Wanders' early years – postmodernism: 'a revelation'

Marcel Wanders trained as an industrial designer in the 1980s, at a time when the design world was still reeling from Memphis. The international group of designers brought together at the end of 1980 by Ettore Sottsass presented its first collection during the Milan Furniture Fair in April 1981 (fig. 1). The furniture and lights, with their eclectic formal language, vibrant colour combinations, exuberant ornamentation, inexpensive materials, such as plastic laminate, and sense of irony were considered an attack on serious design. This was predominantly rooted in modernist ideas and a functionalist language of form. As the term implies, postmodernism emerged after modernism, and rejected both the ethics and aesthetics of that movement. Memphis had enormous international impact, although it failed to make any major inroads in the Netherlands. In architecture, however, Sjoerd Soeters created postmodernist-related designs. The influence of postmodernism can also be seen in the graphic design of figures like Gert Dumbar and Swip Stolk, as well as Czech-born Bořek Šípek, who lived in the Netherlands from 1983 until around 1993, producing exuberant glassware and furniture (fig. 2). The furniture designs of Ed Annink also reveal a kinship with postmodernism. Still, furniture and product design continued to be dominated by the ideal of simple, geometric shapes and sober colours. The Dutch Minimalism of that period was an offshoot of the functionalism that had arisen during the interwar years among the circles of modernists affiliated with the Bauhaus and like-minded designers (fig. 3).[1] After World War II, it was no longer an idealistic movement committed to creating a new, better world: modernism had become a style, far less ideologically driven, although it still retained that positive connotation. Another factor specific to the Netherlands was that, due to scant interest from producers, many designers – including Bruno Ninaber van Eyben, Martijn Wegman and Frans van Nieuwenborg – produced their own designs, and thus created an independent position.[2] This was bolstered by the flourishing subsidy culture and generous government policy, providing designers with commissions. Relatively few Dutch designers were confronted by the gritty reality of surviving in a purely commercial world. In Western Europe, meanwhile, increasing interest in 'design' had spawned the phenomenon of the 'star designer', one who assertively carves out a niche in the commercial world.[3] Philippe Starck, a moderate postmodernist, became its prototype.

Fig. 2 **Overview of the exhibition 'Bořek Šípek' solo show at the Musée des Arts Décoratifs, Lyon (FR), 1987**

1 The term Dutch Minimalism was introduced in 2012 by the Stedelijk Museum's design curators at the museum's reopening in connection to the Design collection presentation. For modernism, see: Christopher Wilk, *Modernism. Designing a New World 1914-1939*, London 2006.

2 'Self-producing' does not always mean that the designer handles the production himself. It can also mean that the designer oversees production, or that the designer outsources part of the production process and assembles the product himself. The essence is that the initiative lies with the designer. A number of self-producing designers were featured in the exhibition and accompanying catalogue *Design in Nederland*, The Hague (De Nederlandse Kunststichting) 1981.

3 From the 1970s on, the term 'design', including all forms of design (from small editions to industrial and graphic design) was increasingly used in non-English-speaking countries to signify product design, with which many designers gathered attention in the media. Also in the Netherlands, the term came into fashion, praising the design of products. Arjen Ribbens used it this way in 2006: 'Now there is design for ordinary things too'. In this article he wrote about designs by Wanders for HE, and by Starck for Princess: Arjen Ribbens, 'Design voor keuken en badkamer', *NRC Handelsblad*, 24 January 2006. In Marlies Philippa et. al., *Etymologisch Woordenboek van het Nederlands*, Amsterdam 2003-2009, design is described as 'industrial design, especially fashionable and striking; striking and fashionable design' [industriële vormgeving, met name modieus en opvallend; opvallend en modieus ontwerp]. It also mentions the use of the term in the Dutch language since 1975. Online consultation (21 September 2013) through the website http://www.etymologiebank.nl/trefwoord/design. See for the hollow term 'design' in Dutch also: Titus Eliëns, *Kunstnijverheid of industriële vormgeving. Dat is de kwestie*, Zwolle 1997, 31.

4 Email from Wanders to the author, 4 September 2013.

5 Peter van Kester, 'Perfectie met pietluttigheid. 'Docent terrible' Dick Lion (Arnhem)', *Items*, (1999) 4, 68-69; quote about about Šípek from the interview with Robert Thiemann and Alexandra Onderwater, 21 and 28 August 2013

Wanders graduated *cum laude* from the department of 3D design at the Institute of the Arts in Arnhem (now ArtEZ) in 1988. Prior to this, he had spent a year at the Academy for Industrial Design in Eindhoven (now Design Academy), but was expelled for being too strong-minded, and several years at the Academy for Applied Arts in Maastricht, part of which he combined with a simultaneous study in Hasselt, Belgium. These diverse training programmes acquainted Wanders with classic modernist (Eindhoven), handcrafted (Maastricht) and more industrial (Hasselt) design, giving him a broad and versatile foundation. Wanders did not come into contact with Memphis until studying at the academy in Hasselt (1983-1985). It was a 'revelation' to discover the existence of a design style so entirely different from what he had seen around him, and to realise that 'design philosophy was not as stable as everyone had led him to believe.'[4] In Arnhem, Wanders was taught by Dick Lion, who was inspired by the postmodern language of form, and was introduced to the work of Bořek Šípek, which he considered 'genius' because it was more 'romantic, warm and detailed'.[5] Traces of the movement's influence can be detected in Wanders' early designs, such as the jewellery (asymmetrical with a combination of various materials) created to mark the tenth anniversary of the Vereniging van Edelsmeden en Sieraadontwerpers [The Association of Goldsmiths and Jewellery Designers] VES and the furniture he designed for his graduation presentation (fig. 4).

While still a student in Arnhem, it was clear that Wanders had a promising future ahead. In 1986, he won two competitions: 'Café Modern' (Nestlé) for an individual coffee experience, and for designs for prizes to be awarded during the 1992 Olympic Games. Wanders also had designs in production with two manufacturers: bowls and dishes with ceramic manufacturer Tichelaar and the *Mobilis* lounge chair

Fig.3 **Overview of the Collection Presentation Design in the Stedelijk Museum with works by Memphis (right) placed next to works of contemporary Dutch Minimalism (left)**

Fig. 4 *Wearable objects*, 1985-1986, made on the occasion of the 10th anniversary of the Society of Silversmiths and Jewellery Designers (VES), aluminum, plastic, collection Museum voor Moderne Kunst, Arnhem (NL)

Fig. 5 *Mobilis* (model F 045), adjustable armchair, 1985, Artifort, Maastricht (NL), pressed wood and metal, painted, rubber, upholstered with wool

Fig. 6 *Ephese*, pitcher/vase, 1987, Tichelaar Makkum (NL), glazed ceramics, cover *Items* magazine (1988) 27

with Artifort (fig. 5). Wanders himself considers *Mobilis* a youthful indiscretion.[6] In fact, it is quite an ingenious design for a lounge chair that can be adjusted to two positions, reclining and upright – but who's going to keep switching between the two? In 1987, *Mobilis* was featured in *Domus*, a highpoint in the career of many designers.[7] Wanders' inventiveness and talent for innovation is also evident in his design for the *Dipstick* (see p. 66) for the Café Modern competition. Despite Nestlé's enthusiasm, the product was never launched on the market. Wanders' graduation project, the white-glazed earthenware pitcher/vase *Ephese*, the design of which references ancient Egypt, graced the cover of the design magazine *Items* (fig. 6).[8] Wanders' graduation collection included a sizeable number of designs ripe for production. In addition to *Ephese*, he designed a lounge chair with a changeable back rest, lights with a folding mechanism in the shade for which a patent was filed, and a display cabinet on a console (fig. 8). Wanders also created more conceptual projects, such as a carpet with LED lighting with built-in sensors that react to the weather, and the *Bad Black Box*, which questions the notion of 'design'.

In 1985, articles about the work of Wanders began appearing in Dutch newspapers and magazines. In an interview in the *Rotterdams Nieuwsblad*, he was extremely candid, stating that although he might not yet be an outstanding designer, he certainly intended to become one – a testament to his boundless ambition and self-assurance that some interpreted as arrogance even then.[9] In the Netherlands, such an attitude is not always greeted with whole-hearted appreciation.

In 1990, after working independently for eighteen months, Wanders joined Landmark Design & Consult, a Rotterdam agency that focused mainly on designs for

6 Wanders called the design 'a youthful sin' in an email to the author, 6 May 2004.

7 'Mobili europei', *Domus*, (July/August 1987) 685, n.p. The chair was featured earlier in the German magazine *MD*, (1987) 6, 46.

8 Noudi Spönhoff, 'Marcel Wanders, een veelbelovende jonge ontwerper', *Items*, 7 (August 1988) 27, cover and pp. 18-21.

9 'Ontwerpen als marathon', *Rotterdams Nieuwsblad*, 27 October 1990. Noudi Spönhoff referred to the critique of arrogance as early as 1988. In the interview for that article, Wanders said: 'I want everything and I want it all to be very good [Ik wil alles en heel erg goed]', Spönhoff 1988, op. cit. (note 8), 18.

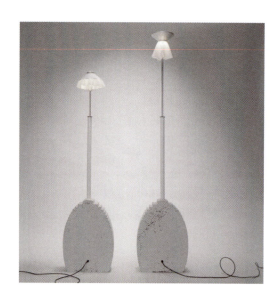

Fig. 7 **Armchair carried out with removable backrest,** 1987-1988 prototype in collaboration with Artifort, metal, leather, fabric by Kvadrat

Fig. 8 **Lamp with concrete base,** 1987-1988, aluminum, microfibre with lycra, metal, plastic, concrete with lava beads

the industrial sector. On his own initiative, Wanders was primarily assigned projects in the cultural sector, yet was keen to broaden his horizons.[10] He had come into contact with Landmark during a competition for a new dinner service for KLM. Landmark won, but was impressed by Wanders' design and took him on to put the finishing touches to their own design. Another of the projects he worked on was a device for pregnancy testing kits commissioned by Organon (fig. 9).

Wanders had been planning to start his own company and, a little over two years later, he did so, but this time in partnership with three colleagues: Joost van Alfen, Joost Alferink and Dienand Christe.[11] The four WAAC's designers (the name is based on the first letters of each surname) called themselves 'design knights': 'We see WAAC's as a company of knights riding through the timeless world landscape of design (...). We are the crown princes of Dutch design that do battle in the international tournament of illusion and dreams.'[12] Dreams have remained a recurrent motif in Wanders' work.

On a personal level, this was a harrowing time for Wanders. His then-girlfriend, Annette, was diagnosed with cancer, and the couple began to research naturopathy. This quest influenced his work for the better, says Wanders, propelling him to attempt to unite very opposite worlds. 'It became clear to me how I could realise my ideals to achieve sustainability and humanist design.'[13]

In 1995, the launch of his own design agency, Wanders Wonders, and a relocation to Amsterdam marked a new phase in his life. Annette was better and they left Rotterdam, the city associated with her illness. A year later, Wanders made his international breakthrough.

The international breakthrough with Droog

In April 1993, Renny Ramakers and Gijs Bakker presented Dutch designs in Milan under the name Droog Design. Earlier that year, Ramakers, art historian and editor-in-chief of the magazine *Industrieel Ontwerpen (Industrial Design)*, had shown several designs in a number of small presentations, including a cabinet by Jan Konings

Fig. 9 **Pregnancy test,** 1990, Organon Teknika, polystyrene

and Jurgen Bey and the *Set Up Shades* by Wanders. With the enormous attention Ramakers garnered with the presentation 'Een middag gewoon doen' (which roughly translates as 'an afternoon of acting normal') that she organised on 28 February 1993 in Paradiso, a music venue in Amsterdam, she realised she was on to something (fig. 10). Ramakers saw a number of Dutch designers beginning to work with a new type of design. Taking a 'back to basics' approach, they distanced themselves not only from the abstract geometry of Dutch Minimalism, but also from the 'design anarchy' of the international postmodern design of the 1980s. Since Memphis, the psychological, symbolic and poetic values of objects had become more important, and would go on to play a vital role in further developments.[14] Ramakers dubbed Wanders' *Set Up Shades*, of which she purchased one of the prototypes for her own use, 'the first signal'.[15]

Ramakers knew that Bakker, a tutor at the academy in Eindhoven, was planning to present work by current and former students in Milan that year, and suggested making a joint presentation. The exhibition they organised in April during the Milan Furniture Fair was a runaway success. Many designs displayed a frugal use of resources, recycled materials and/or typologies, and greater emphasis on the context and the story of a design than the form. The Dutch Design that emerged from this became most noted for being a highly conceptual design movement. Many designs were typified by unorthodox mixtures of materials and techniques and unexpected functions.

Encouraged by their success in Milan, Bakker and Ramakers decided to continue the collaboration and established the Droog Design Foundation in early 1994. Rather than initiating a group of designers or production company, they saw it as a platform to promote Dutch design internationally. To this end, they assembled a collection and organised presentations. The first and oldest design that entered the Droog Design collection was the *Set Up Shades* by Wanders. Ramakers later characterised the designers involved in Droog – Konings, Bey and Wanders, along with Hella Jongerius, Dick van Hoff, Tejo Remy, Richard Hutten and others – as 'those who had discarded Design with a capital "D", design as style,' by which she meant design of the 1980s.[16]

Although they used DMD (Development Manufacturing Distribution) from the outset, the production and distribution of the designs did not run smoothly at first.

[10] Conversation between Wanders and the author, 2 September 2013.

[11] Idem. Joost Alferink had worked for Neonis, a design agency that had also participated in the KLM service competition. Wanders and Alferink met each other while traveling to one of the producers of the in-flight services. In 1992, Wanders contacted him to invite him to join the newly established design agency. Joost van Alfen and Dienand Christe had studied with Wanders in Arnhem. Wanders left in 1995. WAACs (nowadays without the apostrophe) still exists, but without the four founders.

[12] 'We zien WAAC's als een genootschap van ridders die door het tijdloze wereldlandschap van design rijden (...). We zijn de kroonprinsen van het Nederlands design, die strijden in het internationale toernooi van illusie en dromen.', J. Huisman, 'Designridders tussen droom en daad', *De Volkskrant*, 31 October 1992.

[13] Conversation with the author, 2 September 2013. Wanders also referred to this quest in Marieke van Zalingen, 'Het EH&I estafette-interview Jan des Bouvrie & Marcel Wanders', *Eigen Huis & Interieur*, February 2001, 55-57.

[14] Ida van Zijl, *Droog Design 1991-1996*, Utrecht 1997, 102; Renny Ramakers and Gijs Bakker, *Droog Design. Spirit of the Nineties*, Rotterdam 1998, 30; Renny Ramakers, *Droog. A Human Touch*, Amsterdam 2006, 6-11. See also: 'Introduction' in: Renny Ramakers, *Less + More. Droog Design in Context*, Rotterdam 2002, 6-13.

[15] Telephone conversation with the author, 26 August 2013. Quote from: B. van Mechelen, 'Renny Ramakers over Droog Design', *Items* (2004) 6, 43.

[16] Email from Ramakers to the author, 5 October 2013. See also M. Horsham, 'What is Droog?', *Blueprint* (October 1996), 3-6.

Fig. 10 **Presentation 'Een middag gewoon doen', 28 februari 1993 in club Paradiso, with amongst other designs the *Voddenstoel* by Tejo Remy, the *Set Up Shades* (1989) by Wanders and the bookshelves by Konings and Bey.**

Fig. 11 *Knotted Chair* (prototype no.5), lounge chair, design 1995-1996, knotted aramide fibre cord with carbon core, secured with epoxy resin, sand blasted, collection Stedelijk Museum Amsterdam

Fig. 12 **Detail during manufacture of the *Zeppelin*, hanging lamp, 2005, Flos, cocoon, crystal, perspex, steel**

Many designs were only best known through media exposure. Later, Droog solved this by creating a separate, private company to produce part of the collection, as well as by opening shops. Other manufacturers (such as Cappellini and later Moooi) started producing Droog designs. In 1995, Droog began organising projects that focused on a theme, for instance, specific materials or types of objects. Until 1999, Marcel Wanders took part in most of these projects (see pp. 72-73, 78 and 144-145). The first, Dry Tech, organised together with the Aerospace Engineering Faculty of Delft University of Technology, explored the application of ultralight composites. Wanders developed the *Knotted Chair* for this project (fig. 11), a design that garnered enormous attention during its presentation in Milan, in April 1996, and forged his reputation internationally (for a detailed analysis of its design, see pp. 118-125).

The designer pinned up and his work analysed: A main theme and ten sub-themes

By the mid-1990s, every theme that can be identified in Wanders' work had fully evolved. The motto of his company, Wanders Wonders, reveals his positive attitude towards the profession of designer: 'Here to create an environment of love, live with passion and make our most exciting dreams come true.'[17] Contributing to a beautiful, inspiring world, and one that is also sustainable, is integral to Wanders' vision. Wanders' ideal of encouraging users to build a relationship with the product was also an important aspect for Droog, say Ramakers and Bakker.[18] The design must appeal to users through a combination of familiar and surprising aspects that, ideally, invoke different senses to create a 'visual, auditory and kinaesthetic experience'. As early as 1989, Wanders told an interviewer, 'I try to make something familiar'. He often succeeds; commenting on the *Set Up Shades*, trend watcher Li Edelkoort said that the object looks 'as if it should have existed already a long time ago'.[19]

If people build a relationship with a product, they will cherish it and not want to throw it away, which may ultimately lead to greater sustainability than a sparing use of resources and/or recycling. Wanders once said of the *Knotted Chair*, 'I wanted to make a chair that says "I was made with so much love, so much attention, so much care, I will serve you for the rest of your life".'[20] Naturally, this calls for the use of good-quality materials, refraining from fashionable forms and ensuring that the object ages gracefully. Although Wanders' oeuvre is varied and extremely broad, it is difficult to date many of the designs with any certainty. The designer intentionally avoids a datable 'newness', because nothing ages as rapidly as the new.[21] This can be said of the *Card Case* (1994) and *Big Shadow* (1998), for instance, but equally applies to more recent designs, such as the *Sparkling Chair* (2010) and *Carbon Balloon Chair* (2013, see pp. 74, 77, 79 and 162-167).

In addition to the principal theme of sustainability described above, Wanders' work can also be grouped into ten sub-themes; however, given the richness of his work, other motifs can undoubtedly be detected. Designs can, of course, blend traits from several different themes. In Wanders' creative mind so much is going on at once that there are often no clear distinctions, and innumerable developments, at different phases, coexist.

Upcycling memories

Wanders infuses existing shapes, techniques, or objects with new life by utilising them for a new design, such as the natural sponges dipped in liquid porcelain clay and fired to create the *Sponge Vase* (1997, see p. 78), or the *Zeppelin* (fig. 12 and p. 86), for which Wanders 'borrowed' the spray-coated cocoon technique of a designer he much admires, the Italian Achille Castiglioni.[22] A language of form inspired by historical examples can also receive similar treatment. A prime example can be seen in the *New Antiques* series for Cappellini (2005, see p. 87), which references traditional turned wood furniture. In each of these cases, it is crucial that the consumer sees something familiar in the design. Wanders published his manifesto, *War on Design*, to coincide with the launch of his *New Antiques* collection. In the pamphlet, he rebukes designers and an industry that cling to a language of form and production techniques, ones that may have been suited to the early days of the industrial revolution but which Wanders believes are now outdated.[23] Technology should serve humanity, not vice versa, claims Wanders.[24] In today's world, computer-driven machines offer so much more than the simple techniques of the early industrial era, and Wanders appeals to designers to offer this to their audiences as well.[25]

Wanders' interpretation of historical inspirations could be called 'postmodern', although the postmodernism of the 1980s often drew on classical examples. Wanders finds inspiration in a far broader spectrum that includes Rococo and Baroque. Many

17 The motto was published on the endpaper of Paola Antonelli and Yvònne Joris, *Wanders Wonders. Design for a new age*, 's-Hertogenbosch/Rotterdam 1999. Wanders has used the motto since the mid-1990s. Email from Wanders to the author, 10 September 2013.

18 Letter accompanying the book Ramakers 2006 (op. cit. note 14), 3 December 2006.

19 According to Wanders, these three aspects always need to be present in the design, but the ratio can differ. See Marleen Castelein, 'Wanders Wonders: Design voor nu en later,' *Eye. Zicht op trends*, December 1999, 10-11. The interview 'De veelzijdige wereld van de industriële vormgeving. Jonge ontwerpers exposeren bij Stichting ioN', was published in: *Rotterdams Nieuwsblad*, 19 January 1989; for the interview with Li Edelkoort, 'alsof het er allang had moeten zijn', see: Marion van Eeuwen, 'Een innovatieve uitslover', *NRC Handelsblad*, 3 July 2002.

20 Amy Goldwasser, 'Natural Wanders', *ID-magazine*, March/April 2000, 82.

21 Castelein 1999, op. cit. (note 19), 11. Wanders calls his designs 'so unmodern you won't discard them for the next few years, [zó niet-modern dat je ze over een paar jaar zeker nog niet wegdoet]', V. van Vliet, 'Moooi, zo'n snotvaas', *Het Parool*, 7 April 2001.

22 Together with his brother, Pier Giacomo, Achille Castiglioni used this technique to design the *Taraxacum* and the *Gatto* (both in 1960) for Flos, which are both still in production. Flos is also the producer of the *Zeppelin*. During a discussion in 2004, Wanders stated that Castiglioni is 'always looking over his shoulder' [altijd over zijn schouder meekijkt] while designing. Amsterdam, May 2004, Stedelijk Museum CS.

23 http://www.marcelwanders.com/products/seating/new-antiques/. Last consultation 10 September 2013.

24 Marcel Wanders, 'Foreword. The Contemporary Renaissance of Humanism', in: Marcus Fairs, *21st century design. New Design Icons from Mass-Market to Avant-garde*, London 2006, 7.

25 'We have to work for our public and create great value for them', in: Marcel Wanders et al., *Marcel Wanders. Interiors*, New York 2011, 226.

Fig. 14 *Tijdschrift voor een snel vergetende wereld*, 1987-1992 (these ones from 1989), printed glass and marble respectively, screen printed, gold leaf, edition 1

other designers also look to the past. For instance, in her *Comback Chair* (2013) for Kartell, Patricia Urquiola based her design on the English *Windsor Chair*. For Wanders, 'upcycling', as referred to here, is never about recycling materials, which from the 1990's regularly featured in work by designers such as Piet Hein Eek and Bär + Knell.[26]

(Re)discovering archetypes

The use of archetypical shapes can, in fact, be seen as an expression of the aforementioned theme of upcycling. Almost of all Wanders' designs for lights, from the *Set Up Shades* (1989), with its standard white lampshades, to *B.L.O.* (fig. 12), which resembles an old-fashioned flat candlestick, could be considered such an 'archetype'. Wanders claims to 'steal' these shapes 'from our heads', returning them to us in a new design.[27] He is not the only designer with an interest in archetypes: Richard Hutten and Konstantin Grcic are also often associated with this. Their objects tend to be utensils with a restrained, sober design. Wanders refers to the fact that some people, designers among them, reject historical examples, as well as the archetypes and shapes inspired by them, in favour of the new and unknown, as a sort of 'baby face fixation'.[28] The 'constant' dogmatic quest for the new is precisely what he rejects in modernism.

Stories and dialogues

Fig. 12 *B.L.O.*, table lamp, 2001, Flos, polished stainless steel, perspex. Photograph: Flos

From his earliest days as a designer, even while still a student, the story behind a design was vital for Wanders. In 2000, he even said, 'I see design as a way to tell a story'.[29] Knowing those stories is often essential to fully understanding the design. Each issue of the *Tijdschrift voor een snel vergetende wereld* [*Journal for a Rapidly Forgetting World*], a magazine which Wanders produced in an edition of one, from 1987 to 1992, consisted of a square sheet (figs. 14). The cover is partly covered by gold leaf, rendering the text beneath illegible for decades to come, until the gold has worn away.[30] In this way, Wanders expressly weaves the element of time into his work. For the project, he asked the Italian designer Andrea Branzi and philosopher Eric Bolle, among others, to write about things that should never be forgotten. It is precisely this attentiveness to narrative and the concept behind a design that led to the rapid association of Wanders with the conceptual design emerging in the Netherlands at the time. For Wanders, however, the concept or narrative never outweighs the execution, to which he also devotes meticulous attention. The perfectly-realised *Airborne Snotty Vases* (see p. 90) cannot be fully appreciated without knowing that the shape is based on (massively magnified) human snot. Recently, more designers have come to share this interest in narratives and production, as we can see in the catalogue for the exhibition *Telling Tales*, which the Victoria and Albert Museum organised in 2009.[31] Wanders has also begun to tell stories that express his darker side, such as those involving the monsters whose faces are pictured or embroidered on the backrest of the *Monster Chair* (2010, see p. 93). The story he wrote about the piece begins, 'One day I will die...'.[32] Back in 2008, known for his optimism and energy, Wanders declined to hint at any possible darker sides of his personality.[33] The about-face may well be connected to his age and the need to make more personal work; Wanders turned 50 in 2013 – a moment he believes is ripe for reflection.

Since the 1980s, Wanders has pursued the concept of the dialogue between different elements, for which he uses the Japanese term 'haiku'.[34] This may echo the combination of different decorative elements, as seen in the *Patchwork Plates* for Tichelaar (2003, see pp. 94-95), or three-dimensional shapes, found in the *Couple* vase and *3D Haikus*, a kind of miniature still life featuring Wanders' designs (see pp. 103, 105). The dialogue entered into by the different elements emboldens the combinations with richer meanings and associations.

26 Eek became known for his scrap wood furniture, Piet Hein Eek et al., *Boek. Piet Hein Eek 1990-2006*, Eindhoven 2006. Bär + Knell use recycled plastic from packaging for their furniture. Exh. cat. *Plastics + Design*, Darmstadt (Museum Künstlerkolonie Mathildenhöhe) 1997-1998.

27 'Quoted in: P. Doze, 'Space M. Wanders', *Intramuros*, (2002) 102, 72. Wanders already talks about the use of archetypes in: 'Hogeschool voor Beeldende Kunsten, Arnhem. Lamp en fauteuil', exh.cat. *Nieuwe ontwerpers afstudeerwerk 1988*, Rotterdam 1989, 25.

28 Bas van Lier, 'Producten voor de eeuwigheid. Eternally Yours strijdt tegen verspilling van massaproductie', *Adformatie*, (14 August 1997) 38; Antonelli and Joris 1999, op. cit. (note 17), 22.

29 Robert Thiemann, 'Spinner of Tales', *Frame*, (2000) 17, 44.

30 Marzee invitation to the exhibition 'Marcel Wanders', Nijmegen 1988: 'The guest editor writes about what he would like to save for this world'.

31 The catalogue only features one of Wanders' *Giant Bells*, not the most obvious choice when referring to narratives in his *oeuvre*: Gareth Williams, *Telling Tales*, London 2009, 68.

32 http://www.marcelwanders.com/products/seating/monster-chair/ . Last consultation 10 September 2013.

33 Robert Vuijsje, 'Ontwerper Marcel Wanders. "Een stoel gaat niet over zitten"', *Dagblad De Pers*, 5 December 2008; conversation between Wanders and the author, 18 September 2013.

34 The catalogue of the exhibition 'De Oogst' (The Harvest) refers to Wanders' work as 'Dutch haiku'. It describes the haiku as a 'literary form in which the highest form of simplicity merges with the deepest thoughts'. It suggests that this imbues Wanders' work with its current 'poetic orientation', exh. cat. *De Oogst*, Amsterdam (Stedelijk Museum Amsterdam) 1993, n.p. See also the essay by Jennifer Hudson in this book, note 6 on p. 44.

Fig. 15 *Lace Table*, 1997, commissioned by Droog, created during the Dry Tech II project, epoxy fixated Swiss lace, sand blasted

Fig. 16 **Marcel Wanders and Erwin Olaf, publicity photo from the series *Inside the Box*, 2012, for Moooi. This photograph shows the *Random Light* by Bertjan Pot (2001)**

35 The publication *European Design* calls this Neo-Decorative Design: R. Craig Miller, 'Neo-Decorative Design', in: R. Craig Miller, Penny Sparke and Catherine McDermott, *European Design Since 1985. Shaping the New Century*, London/New York 2008, 226-245.

36 Even Renny Ramakers, an early admirer of Wanders' work, says she still values Wanders as a designer, but the exuberant decoration of, for example, the Kameha Grand Hotel in Bonn is just 'too much' for her: 'Decoration can be very beautiful, but when you're surrounded by these ornamental patterns – in the curtains, in the flooring, on lamps and other things, it can become too much of a good thing. It's just not for me', as she stated in an interview by telephone with the author, 26 August 2013.

37 Annemiek Leclaire, 'Marcel Wanders. Meer is meer', *Vrij Nederland*, (2013) 15, 71.

The depth of surface

In several designs created in the 1990s, the surface and the construction become one through the use of epoxy. In both the *Knotted Chair* and the *Lace Table* (fig. 15) the surface has a three-dimensional aspect, imparting the design with depth. This same three-dimensionality is more powerfully present in the *Stone Chair* (2001, see p. 105) with its skin of pebbles, and in the mosaic tiles developed by Wanders in collaboration with Bisazza for one of the breathtaking 'Swarovski Crystal Palace' presentations in Milan (2008, see p. 109). This fascination for a skin that is also a construction is something Wanders shares with designers like Bertjan Pot. It was therefore hardly a coincidence when Wanders added Pot's *Random Light* (fig. 16) to the collection of the Moooi furniture brand, for which he is the art director. The lamp is created by hand-wrapping glass fibre soaked in epoxy around a balloon. It was the first of Pot's designs to be produced in a larger edition for the market.

Since 2002-2003, Wanders has increasingly incorporated two-dimensional decoration into his designs. He initially used bright flower motifs, such as those on the exterior of the *Stonehouses* in the Interpolis building in Tilburg (2002, see p. 110). In recent years, his patterns have become a more abstract ornamentation that references historic styles or diverse cultures but never literally derives from them, or even connects with one specific example. In the new millennium, Wanders is not alone in his interest in the surface and use of decoration. Tord Boontje and Studio Job are other well-known representatives of Het Nieuwe Ornament (The New Ornament), or Neo-Decorative Design.[35] Boontje largely explores flower and plant motifs, from time to time integrating off-beat, slightly menacing elements like sharp spines in what at first appear to be cute patterns for domestic textiles (fig. 17). Studio Job has evolved an idiosyncratic language of form that features insects and all kinds of utensils. Neither designer, however, ever combines as many disparate elements as does Wanders. These combinations of different ornamentation in Wanders' interior projects, which can be a little overwhelming, often provoke the critique that Wanders' designs are over the top, or kitsch – criticism that seems to originate from a long-standing discussion on decoration, ornament and taste, as the essay by Marjan Groot proposes.[36] At other times, Wanders has been reproached with restricting himself to styling – uncritically layering existing designs with decoration – yet his use of ornament far surpasses the simple gesture of adding decoration; the surface, the skin, is an inextricable and indispensible part of his designs.[37] Similar motifs frequently reappear in new designs, but this is true of many designers – take Studio Job's insect pattern, for example, which can be found on myriads of products.

Quiet things

One may not automatically expect to see designs with a tranquil or 'quiet', almost timeless, sensibility in Wanders' oeuvre. These designs are not the spectacular designs for which he is known, but functional, industrially-produced objects such as the *Card Case*, *Lucy* candlestick (1999, see p. 111) and the complete *Wanders Wonders Lighting* collection (fig. 18). The greater part of these products were designed in the second half of the 1990s, but the *Wattcher* (2009, see p. 112), a device that enables the

Fig. 17 **Tord Boontje,** *Sleeping Rose* interior fabric, 2005, Kvadrat, printed Trevira cs

Fig. 18 *Wanders Wonders Lighting Collection*, 1997, Wanders Wonders, some designs are included in the collection of Moooi in 2001, metal, PVC/viscose laminate

monitoring of one's own electricity consumption, is also at home in this category. In terms of their formal language, such objects appear highly functionalist, although Wanders distances himself from this view. Because he considers functionality an integral aspect of utensils and appliances, it is never an aspect that Wanders takes as a starting point for design.[38]

However, offering a conclusive explanation of the objects that belong to this portion of his oeuvre is far from easy. The fact is, in the Netherlands, it is precisely this type of design that, as a later offshoot of modernism, still holds currency. As such, Wanders knows it all too well, and may have been more influenced by this kind of design than he is willing to admit. I do not rule out the possibility that these designs may be a response to the enormous emphasis placed on the concept in the mid-1990s, and that the decoration of the last decade may also be a reaction to it.

Humanising the product

In the face of the impersonal, industrially-produced mass product, many people long for the unique. Using crafts causes that no two pieces are exactly the same. Variation can also be created in the final product by selecting a production process that will automatically result in differentiation, such as with the *Sponge Vase* (see p. 78), whose shape is defined by the particular sponge that is used, or by giving the client the possibility of adding something personal to the product itself. The latter approach, also known as customisation, may mean offering the client a large number of variants from which to make a selection (such as the covers of the *Bottoni* sofas, see p. 113); allowing people to add something of their own, such as picking a photo for the *Lijstbroches* (Frame Brooches, fig. 19); or letting them create their own content for the legs of the *Flare table* (a drawing, a collection of pebbles, or any number of objects can be placed

[38] Conversation between Wanders and the author, 2 September 2013. As early as 1989 Wanders pleaded for more attention for other aspects of design than just function, in: Marcel Wanders, 'Vertelling van kinderen en badwater' (1985), *De vierde Dimensie. Bulletin voor de afdeling 3D Design* 1 (1989) 1, 30. 'Functionality is highly overrated', in: S. Moreno, *Marcel Wanders. Behind the Ceiling*, Berlin 2009, 165.

within its hollow, transparent legs). Wanders is very aware of this need to 'humanise' the product, not only by enhancing its individuality but also by imbuing the design with more emotion.

The hidden engineer

Although the profession of industrial designer demands considerable research, not to mention the testing of materials, techniques and constructions, Wanders prefers to present himself rather as a storyteller than a kind of engineer. Nonetheless, he has an innate urge to innovate, despite that he does not display this as clearly in his work as, for example, Joris Laarman, nor make it his prime focus, as does Ron Arad. Innovation can relate to a new type of product, or to developing or applying new materials and techniques. Wanders was one of the first designers to use the SLS three-dimensional print technique for a product rather than simply a prototype. In 1999, he designed the *SLS vase* (see p. 114) that exploits the technique to its fullest potential. In his interiors, Wanders also strives for elements that surprise and innovate. He developed a wall that 'breathes' with the help of fans for the Mandarina Duck Flagship Store in London (2002, see p. 115). The mannequins 'breathe' as well, giving the design an extra, human element.

Wanders' best-known innovations can be found in his use of materials, for instance, the cord with the carbon core used in the *Knotted Chair*. Since 1995, permeating various materials with epoxy has been a constant thread throughout his work. Wanders uses this application in the *Lace Table* (1997), *Crochet Table* (2001), *Crochet Chair* (2006) and *Topiaries* (fig. 20). In 2004, he added the *Carbon Chair* (fig. 21) to this collection, which also employs this method. In collaboration with Bertjan Pot, Wanders made the design of the *Carbon Copy* – the form of which Pot had

Fig. 19 **Lijstbroches,** brooches, 1987, commisioned by Galerie Ra, painted metal, gold leaf, plastic

Fig. 20 **Overview of Wanders' solo exhibition *Daydreams* at the Philadelphia Museum of Art, 2009, including two *Topiaries Sid* (2007)**

Fig. 21 **From left to right Bertjan Pot in collaboration with Marcel Wanders,** *Carbon Chair* **(2004), Moooi, Bertjan Pot,** *Random Chair* **(2003) and Bertjan Pot,** *Carbon Copy* **(2003), epoxy fixated carbon filament, collection Stedelijk Museum Amsterdam.**

Fig. 22 *Turned Arm Sunglasses*, 2013, **Marks & Spencer, polycarbonate**

based on *DSR* by Charles & Ray Eames, ready for production. To my knowledge, it is the first item of furniture in which 'naked' unwoven carbon filament is used.[39]

The theatre of making

Over the last fifteen years, crafts have become increasingly popular in designer circles. Previously, they were often dismissed as old-fashioned or frumpy; as of late, the use of rediscovered crafts like knitting, crocheting and painting by hand has, in fact, become a show of progressiveness. This renewed interest in crafts goes hand in hand with a search for humanity, variation, the unusual, or a local counterpart in a globalised world.[40] In his influential book, *The Craftsman*, Richard Sennett described craftsmanship, which is often associated with crafts, as the desire to do something well 'for its own sake'; quality plays a key role in this.[41] For Wanders, the reason behind using craft techniques is generally to make his work more human (which Wanders refers to as 'humanist', to distinguish it from the purely industrial state).[42] Wanders is more concerned with the result than the activity – it is vital that no two specimens of the same design are exactly alike. Once again, this vision is best exemplified by the *Knotted Chair*. The *Crochet Chair*, *Crochet Table* and *Topiaries* are also made entirely by hand (see pp. 138-139), a process in which macramé sections are melded together on a polystyrene core and impregnated with epoxy. Once the design has hardened, the core is removed. The objects are produced in a limited edition and distributed under

Fig. 23 **Candle (with Moooi products),** 2009, **Target, candle wax**

Fig. 24 **JVC building in Mexico City, design, 2003, not executed**

the Personal Editions label. In his more industrial work, Wanders sometimes tries to achieve the same personal attributes. For example, several variants from the *Cyborg* chairs collection by *Magis* are sold with handwoven wicker backrests (2010, see p. 142). In combination with the polycarbonate structure, it exemplifies the marriage of high and low tech, echoing the nature of the cyborg, a fusion of man and machine.

Professional doll's house

Experimenting with scale is one of Wanders' favourite ways of giving people an extraordinary experience. He often plays with a combination of miniaturised and magnified shapes: one can peer into the doll's house from the outside, or gaze out at the great 'big' world from inside, like Alice in Wonderland. Different elements appear in his work in at least four categories of scale. Two examples of these are the turned wood (table) leg and the bell with (or without) clapper. Examples of the first (from small to large) are the legs of a pair of sunglasses designed for Marks & Spencer (fig. 22), a candle for *Target* (fig. 23), the *Calvin* lamp (2007, see p. 159) and the pillars in the Mondrian Hotels in Miami (2008, see pp. 146-147) and Doha (2014, see p. 47).[43] The bell can be seen in a name placeholder-cum-Christmas tree decoration for Target (2009), a special edition powder compact for Cosme Decorte (2013, see p. 153), the *Bell Lamp* for Moooi (2013) and gigantic, hand-painted bells like the *Bella Bettina* (2007, see p. 179), that can double as a lamp. In the case of the shape of the *Egg Vase*, the scale has even expanded in tandem with the dimension of the architecture; the design for the JVC apartment complex in Mexico City (figs. 24) has a similar shape but has not yet been built. By using repetition, Wanders creates instant recognition of, and it is one of the ways in which Wanders accomplishes his principal objective – building a lasting relationship between product and user, which in turn promotes sustainability. Given that familiar typologies are also at play here (that refer, respectively, to historical examples and an archetype), recognition occurs on two levels, at least for those familiar with his work.

[39] There are earlier examples of the use of 'naked' carbon (for example Alberto Meda's *LightLight* from 1987), but those always involve woven mats. A seating object by Matthias Bengtsson from 2002 features a very loosely woven mat, resembling the *Carbon Chair*. See Gareth Williams, *The Furniture Machine. Furniture Since 1990*, London 2006, 103.

[40] For the use of crafts by Dutch designer, see: Ingeborg de Roode, 'Altes Handwerk und Niederländische Designer der Gegenwart / Oude ambachten en hedendaagse Nederlandse ontwerpers', in: Nicole Uniquole (ed.), *Dutch Design. Exzellentes Handwerk am Hofe / Uitmuntend ambacht aan het hof*, Dessau 2012, 160-162.

[41] Richard Sennett, *The Craftsman*, London 2008.

[42] In *Behind the Ceiling*, Wanders writes about 'the humanization of design', op. cit. (note 38), 270. For 'humanist', see J. Temmen, 'Marcel Wanders', *Schöner Wohnen*, May 2013, 143.

[43] The candle for Target comes in a variety of models: both De Bijenkorf (2008) and Marks & Spencer (2011) have had models in their collections.

Unexpected turn

It has often been written, and said, that humour is a key aspect of many Droog Design objects.[44] I believe that to be a bit of an exaggeration. On the whole, the intention is more to catch the user off guard, sometimes because a discrepancy arises between our senses and our assumptions. It is the difference between a burst of laughter and a smile. Wanders also occasionally gets people to smile. The designer himself uses the expression 'The Unexpected Welcome', which often accompanies Moooi presentations. In the *Nomad Carpet* (figs. 25), part of the design can also be folded to serve as a back support, making sitting on the ground far more comfortable; the *VIP Chair* (2000, see p. 155) turns out to possess wheels, which remain invisible, hidden by the loose fabric covering the legs; the *B.L.O.* lamp (2001, see fig. 12) has no switch because one must turn it on and off by blowing; and the *Dressed* cutlery (fig. 26), is decorated only on the back, so that the pattern is felt before it is seen.

Changes in the new millennium

Around 2000, Wanders' professional life gathered momentum. In 1999, he began to expand his sphere of work to include interior design. Wanders had already worked on projects that went beyond furniture design, such as an assignment in Oud-Beijerland on which he collaborated with Jeanne van Heeswijk, although Wanders did not consider it a fully-fledged interior commission. As Wanders began to feel ready, as if by coincidence, he was invited to work on a number of commissions. Firstly, for the Lunch Lounge of the Co van der Horst furniture store in Amstelveen (1999, see p. 172),

Fig. 25 *Nomad Carpet*, 1998, Cappellini, wool, wood.

Fig. 26 *Dressed*, cutlery, 2011, Alessi, pressed and polished stainless steel

rapidly followed by the VIP Room for the Dutch pavilion by architects MVRDV at the World's Fair 2000 in Hannover (see p. 174).⁴⁵ Occasionally, furniture designs arose in the context of a particular project, such as the *VIP Chair* designed for the World's Fair pavilion, and the *New Antiques* series, which evolved while working on the restaurant project at The Hotel on Rivington (2005, see pp. 176-177).

The next radical progression was the founding of the Moooi label, which Wanders started in 2001, together with Casper Vissers. At first, Vissers distributed a collection of lights designed by Wanders through his company, Vissers Design, in the Netherlands. When they decided to launch the series on the international market, and wanted to work with other designers, they established a separate company. Having gained logistics and technical production experience with his own company, Lensvelt B.V., which focused chiefly on the project market, Hans Lensvelt also became involved. Wanders became the art director for Moooi. In this role, he not only creates numerous designs but also selects notable designers – among them, Jurgen Bey, Studio Job, Jasper Morrison and Ross Lovegrove – and gives the latest generation of designers a chance to have their designs mass-produced in larger editions. Among these are Maarten Baas, Bertjan Pot, Front (fig. 27), Jaime Hayon, Nika Zupanc and Osko & Deichmann. The young designers readily acknowledge the boost this gave their careers.⁴⁶ The company rapidly became a success and, thanks in part to the support of B&B Italia, an Italian furniture manufacturer that became co-owner of Moooi in 2006, was able to develop its vision – despite the crisis – into an annual turnover of 20 million euros.⁴⁷ One might say that Moooi assumed the position held by Cappellini until some eight years ago. Cappellini was renowned for being an interior label that hosted an imposing presentation each year at the Milan Furniture Fair, bristling with a plethora of new and innovative designs by emerging and well-known designers. But Moooi avoids falling into the trap that almost cost Cappellini its head: presenting designs not yet production-ready, most of which fail to ever make it onto the market.⁴⁸

Moooi also holds remarkable presentations with spectacular showpieces during the opening of presentations in Milan, like the *Happy Hour Chandelier* (2005) (figs. 28), which featured Wanders' then-girlfriend, choreographer Nanine Linning, pouring champagne for the guests while hanging upside down from a chandelier. For many design purists, the following year's presentation, with semi-clad, well-muscled males in the role of Snow White's seven dwarves, also was going too far. I can see the reason for such a reaction, but Wanders has a consummate understanding of the spirit of the times which, as we all know, is driven by entertainment and image. In a masterly way he uses all theatrical means available to him. In the most recent presentation titled 'Unexpected Welcome', meticulously styled Moooi interiors were combined with autonomous work by the photographer Erwin Olaf. And to make the festive opening an even more celebratory occasion, the second (and last) Frame Moooi Award was presented. The presentation – the talk of the town in Milan – has been nominated for the prestigious Rotterdam Design Prize 2013. Wanders designs everything, from big events like this one to himself, appearing almost always in his usual impeccably tailored suit with an open-necked white shirt and often sporting his own *Rainbow Necklace*.⁴⁹

Fig. 27 **Marcel Wanders and Erwin Olaf, publicity photo from the series *Inside the Box*, 2012, for Moooi. This photograph shows the *Chess Table* by Front (2009)**

44 For instance: Michelle Ogundehin, 'Droog Design's dry wit', *Blueprint*, 1994, September 51: 'Droog Design aren't afraid of humour, but clarity and simplicity are still the key factors'.

45 Conversation between Wanders and the author, 14 August 2013.

46 Emails to the author by Osko & Deichmann, Pot and Zupanc, 17 September 2013.

47 Initially, B&B became owner for 50 per cent. This has been reduced to 25 per cent today. The remaining 75 per cent is in the hands of Wanders and Vissers. Hans Lensvelt has left the company. The cooperation with B&B is important for distribution and technique. Conversation with Casper Vissers, 26 August 2013.

48 At Moooi, Marcel Wanders makes decisions based on a creative vision, and Casper Vissers from a commercial vision. Together they decide which designs will be added to the collection. Prior to that, the design will have been thoroughly discussed with Bart Schilder, head of production development, among others. Interview by telephone with Casper Vissers, 26 August 2013, and Bart Schilder, 25 July 2013.

49 'I design myself as well' [Ik geef mezelf ook vorm], in: Vuijsje 2008, op. cit. (note 33). At the award ceremony for the prize for *Dipstick* in 1986, Wanders already wore a suit: H. Kool, 'Het individuele koffiedrinken overtuigend aangepakt en opgelost', *NRC Handelsblad*, 22 March 1986.

Fig. 28 **First appearance of Nanine Linning in the** *Happy Hour Chandelier* **in the presentation of Moooi in Milan during the Furniture Fair 2005**

Fig. 29 **Marcel Wanders and Erwin Olaf, publicity photo from the series** *Double Portraits*, **2002, for Moooi. In the photograph, the** *Light Shade Shade* **by Jurgen Bey (1999)**

But Moooi does not solely owe its success to the quality of the collection and these mediagenic displays. The publicity photographs the company uses, for which Wanders also acts as art director, are a vital part of the success story. From the outset, Wanders worked intensively with photographer Erwin Olaf. The fruits of this collaboration comprise an intriguing series, like the first group of images in which nude models (and not only svelte young people, but also older and less streamlined models) are photographed with products in eye-catching poses (fig. 29).

Since then, Wanders has been responsible for the art direction of photography for products by other brands. For Alessi's *Dressed* collection of tableware, he developed a photo series with traditional porcelain figurines. For the series of cookware, he devised a concept using animals, and for the Magis *Cyborg* chair collection, he created manipulated images of the human body fused with appliances (see p. 142). In each of these images, Wanders' desire to tell stories is always evident. There is never an image in which only the product is present; Wanders continually includes other elements to fuel connections and dialogues.

Even in the early days of his career, Wanders understood the power of the image and the importance of good photography. With this in mind, he added a photographer to his staff in 2006, and has since created a number of publicity shots with her. Wanders increasingly uses his own likeness in his work, in the belief that he should not hide behind his work. A degree of vanity is, however, nothing strange. In 2002, Wanders posed as a variety artiste of the 1920s for the cover of the French journal *Intramuros*, with slick-backed hair and a golden clown nose (which was, in fact, a necklace he had designed for the collection Chi ha paura....?).[50] Thus the 'Nosé portrait' was born, and began leading a life of its own, appearing in an abstracted version in textiles and all kinds of interior accessories. In many of his projects, Wanders follows in the footsteps of Philippe Starck who, since the 1980s, gave his products a human face by bestowing upon them names of people. Starck also threw himself into the public arena by playfully using his body to grace the covers of his books. He was an excellent example for Wanders. The admiration is mutual, as Starck's business partner once observed in an interview.[51]

One of the most notable design issues of recent years has been design's relationship to the visual arts. Around the year 2000, the art market began to take an interest in various designers' more autonomous objects, created in small editions or as unique pieces. In the wake of the Internet bubble, the art market became fairly overheated, and collectors started shifting their attention to more affordable objects.[52] Designers such as Ron Arad and Marc Newson were brought to the art market. Wanders had always created objects in limited editions, in parallel with his industrial work. Initially he marketed these under the name of his company, Wanders Wonders, and from 2007 as Personal Editions. In that year, at the height of the market just before the crisis hit, Wanders organised a large-scale presentation of this part of his oeuvre during the Milan Furniture Fair (see p. 136). It included works such as the *Bells*, *Crochet* products, *One Minutes* and *Pizzo Carrara Bench* (see p. 143). The collection reflected a more experimental and personal facet of his work, and offered an easier way to experiment than those works that were mass-produced and in large editions. Many of these editions have found uses in Wanders' interior projects. During this time, particularly when the credit crisis exploded, mounting criticism was levelled at the sometimes costly objects, although Studio Job, for example, seems to be more heavily targeted than Wanders himself.

Over the last few years, a clear movement towards a broadening of Wanders' body of work can be detected, broadening his scope from sculptural objects for specific interior projects and towards the visual arts – Wanders considers the *Virtual Interiors* he creates digitally to be autonomous work – and architecture. Even as a student, Wanders believed that art and design were inextricably entwined, and the step towards the visual arts will not be difficult for him to make.[53] As early as 2000, he expressed that he 'would be excited (...) by [wanting] to design a building'.[54] In the meantime, design proposals for several buildings have been completed; now its is a case of waiting for it to actually be built.

Wanders' architectural ambitions also echo those of Starck, whose first building was realised in the late 1980s. It is in the nature of major designers to constantly search for new creative directions. We will probably see many such new steps as Wanders' trajectory unfolds. He has just embarked on an MBA, wishing to expand his business acumen and, possibly, in its wake, more artistic freedom. Despite the fact that, as we have seen, Wanders shares connections with other designers, there is no doubt that he will continue to pursue his own inimitable path, linking innovative and exuberant designs to high-grade execution and inventive ways of immersing his designs in the lives of as many people as possible. Positioning himself as a 'people's designer', Wanders sets an example for younger generations.

50 Doze 2002, op. cit. (noot 27), 70-77.

51 Wanders said in 2003: 'Just like Philippe Starck I want to change things playfully' [Net als Philippe Starck wil ik spelend de dingen veranderen], A. Ribbens, '"Met een kleine ambitie kom je nergens". Industrieel vormgever Marcel Wanders wil spelend de dingen veranderen', *NRC Handelsblad*, 24 July 2003. In 2008 Wanders called Starck 'the best designer', Vuijsje 2008, op. cit. (note 33). John Hitchcox: 'For years Philippe has been telling me that Marcel is the next Philippe Starck', in: L. Tischler, 'Moooi fabulous', *Fast Company*, (2008) 129, 107.

52 Sophie Lovell, *Limited Edition. Prototypen, Unikate und Design-Art-Möbel*, Basel/Boston/Berlin 2009, 225.

53 Johan van Uffelen, 'Het ik-tijdperk in de koffie. Boxtelnaar Marcel Wanders wint prijs met de Dipstick', *Brabants Dagblad*, 22 March 1986.

54 Caroline Kruit, 'De uitdaging van de tijd', *Detail in architectuur*, June 2000, 13. Wanders said in 2008 that he would like to do something about the placement of windmills. With that, he comes close to his first love: when he was in school, he wanted to become a landscape architect. In 2011 Wanders voiced his ambition to design a mosque: J. Scelfo, 'Marcel Wanders on Designing Upbeat Tableware', *The New York Times*, 16 March 2011.

Decoration, Imagination, Seduction

The Work of Marcel Wanders Through Narratives on Ornament and Taste

Over 25 years, the work of Marcel Wanders has become richly themed. Amidst this richness, his label Moooi operates as a provocative statement about beauty. In the history of design, thinking about beauty means thinking about ornament, colour and shape, to which are coupled judgments about taste and morality; Wanders determines his position in the face of these judgments.

Decorative, Imaginative and Seductive – for myself, the positioning of Wanders' work can be found within this categorisation. Firstly, the work is decorative owing to Wanders' love of ornament; he breathes ornamentation. With orderly structures he overlays the floors, walls and ceilings of interiors with leafy patterns and tendrils, stylised and barely recognisable as foliage. They are Wanders' versions of arabesques and Moresque motifs, which he renders in a palette of white, grey, black, gold and yellow (fig. 1).

Fig. 1 **Villa Moda, clothing store, Manama (BH), 2009**

'Our audience expects more from us, we cannot be engineers, we cannot only be smart, we have to be life poets, we have to dream wonders, and we have to be majestic magicians.'

Arabesques impart the work with an historical layering of cross-cultural contacts between the Arabic world and Southern and Western Europe. If I had to think of a timeless reference, I would go to Edgar Allan Poe, the master of psychological Gothic suspense and a true aesthete. For Poe, the Arabesque contrasts dramatically with the tasteless American style of decor. In his semi-humorous essay 'Philosophy of Furniture', written in 1840 and published in the literary *Burton's Gentleman's Magazine*, he describes his ideal interior in a sphere of meditation and intimacy, as a dream setting or unconscious/conscious space and – because of arabesques – an oasis of delight.[1] In sensual terms, Poe places colour, ornament, texture and light in opposition to the simple, straight line. Ornament must synthesise clarity and decoration in an orderly structure with motifs that are 'exceptionally arabesque'. In other words, it must refrain from depictions of flowers or other recognisable objects. Arabesques with crimson, gold and silver-grey for curtains and wallpaper are ethereal. Poe might have immersed himself in this enchantment of Wanders' interiors and come upon his beloved shade of red in the regal refuge of the tulip chairs (fig. 2). This enchantment converges with the melancholy of memories and snatches of recollections from a time long past, or perhaps a faded youth; an *'à la recherche effect'* that nudges its way among old things and objects to nestle between the new designs in the Moooi showrooms in Amsterdam and London (fig. 3). The interiors allow us to experience ornament, shapes and colours at first hand; images and words simply do not suffice.

Wanders and Poe are not alone in their love of ornamentation. Ornamentation is part of design, regardless of whether it has been the subject of discussions of taste over the centuries. Even today, it is impossible to imagine a situation 'after taste', as a

1 Edgar Allan Poe, 'Philosophy of Furniture', in: *The Complete Tales and Poems of Edgar Allan Poe*, Harmondsworth 1984 (1840), 462-466. Online in the journal: http://www.eapoe.org/works/essays/philfurn.htm.

2 K. Kleinman, J. Merwood-Salisbury, L. Weinthal (eds.), *After Taste. Expanded Practice in Interior Design*, New York, 2012.

3 M. Douglas, 'Bad Taste in Furnishing', in: *Thought Styles. Critical Essays on Good Taste*, London 1996, 50–76; P. Bourdieu, *Distinction. A Social Critique of the Judgement of Taste*, London/New York 1984.

4 Charles Dickens, *Hard Times. An authoritative text, backgrounds, sources, and contemporary criticism*, New York 1966 (eds. G. Ford, & S. Monod), 1–6. For an analysis of the text by Dickens, see: K.J. Fielding, 'Charles Dickens and the Department of Practical Art', in: *The Modern Language Review*, XLVIII (1953), 270–277.

5 Dickens, op. cit. (note 4), 6.

6 Cited in A. Friedman, 'People Who Live in Glass Houses: Edith Farnsworth, Ludwig Mies van der Rohe, and Philip Johnson', in: *Woman and the Making of the Modern House: A Social and Architectural History*, New Haven/London 2006, 126–159, 141.

recent book on interior design concludes.² Notions of taste vary from culture to culture but are always discriminating. Statements on matters of taste are bound up with differences between social classes and about what is ugly, and unacceptable.³ Wanders' design reveals choices that were also considered problematic in the past. In 1854, in his serialised novel *Hard Times*, Charles Dickens parodies a debate about 'false principles in design' in which architects and designers disputed the use of ornament and styles of the past.⁴ The debate pertains to the design of industrial products and wishes to cast museum collections as educators of taste. Dickens describes how working-class children in a rapidly industrialising middle England are taught in accordance with the latest methods: their education is confined to learning hard facts that clearly reflect reality. In this vision, ornament is dangerous because it can distract from that reality. The school inspector ridicules a room with a wallpaper patterned with representations of horses because, in actuality, it is impossible for a horse to walk up and down the walls of a room. But the poor girl Sissy does not see the problem because she grew up with imagination. Her father is a clown. To Sissy, carpets with a pattern of flowers are pretty, making her imagine, or fancy, beautiful flowers that exist in reality. The inspector, however, wants her to forget about the word 'fancy', crying 'You don't walk upon flowers in fact; you cannot be allowed to walk upon flowers in carpets.' For the inspector, true taste lies in the abstraction of geometric shapes, combinations of circles and squares and the like, in primary colours. These are '(...) mathematical figures which are susceptible of proof and demonstration. (...). This is fact. This is taste.'⁵

Dickens contrasts individual feelings with normative judgments. Wanders also understands the importance of imagination and the failings of a 'matter-of-fact' outlook. His alter-ego clown face with its gold-plated nose encourages the experience of a horse lamp, table pig and wall-bird-as-artwork as transcending the everyday and attaining the theatrical (fig. 4). Wanders has no use for pedantic taste inspectors such as those sketched by Dickens, and Poe would savour the wall-bird-as-artwork as a decorative element in the interior.

The morality of design has many variants. The most extreme example is the Western rejection of ornament by modernism from 1900; a trace of that criticism

Fig. 2 **Computer image with *Tulip Chairs*, 2010, Cappellini, metal, polyester, textile**

Fig. 4 **The White House of Moooi in The Dock's White Building in London, 2010, with amongst other designs the** Horse Lamp **and** Pig Table **by Front,** Smoke Chairs **by Maarten Baas, the** Emperor **hanging lamp by Neri & Hu and the** Corks **by Jasper Morrison**

can be detected in Dickens' story. But this modernism is also critiqued. A century after Dickens, in *House Beautiful* magazine, a female contributor wrote of the compulsive sterility and lack of ornamentation of the glass house built by Mies van der Rohe between 1945 and 1951 for the prominent physician Edith Farnsworth in Plano, Illinois. In an admonishing tone, the writer compares design, politics and life: '(…) if we can be sold on accepting dictators in matters of taste and how our homes are to be ordered, our minds are certainly well prepared to accept dictators in other departments of life.'[6] While interiors without adornment may not spark judgments about ornamentation, opinions on matters of taste continue to exist. The modernist design of this house is dogmatic and denies the occupant's individual sensibility. Modernism as a principle of style suffocates, and all too rapidly deteriorates into fundamentalism. Wanders is no modernist eschewing illusory imagination and seduction; he celebrates individuality and subjectivity. Moreover, he turns the reality of things upside down by manipulating materials: the delicate, unstructured lacework of his fragile *Crochet Table* is hardened into shape by synthetic resin (fig. 5).

The power of Wanders' illusion of design is also that of the story *La Petite Maison* by Jean-François de Bastide of 1758. The novella narrates a tale of seduction: the protagonist seduces a lady through the sumptuous decor of his Petite Maison, adorned with the latest, costliest furniture and furnishings. The woman is dazzled by the opulent display of artistry and workmanship of designers and artists who actually existed at the time. Although she attempts to resist the Marquis' attentions, as she encounters one room lovelier than the last, she is convinced that she has entered a *'temple du génie et du goût'*. On reaching a boudoir in which mirrored walls and ceiling

Fig. 3 **Moooi showroom in London during the London Design Week, September 2013, with amongst other designs the** Miyake **floor lamp by Arihiro Miyake, the** Smoke Chair **by Maarten Baas and the** Soft Clock **by Kiki van Eijk**

7 M. Delon (ed.), *Vivant Denon, Point de lendemain suivi de Jean-François de Bastide, La Petite Maison*, Paris 1995, 113, 115-116.

8 J. Bernard, *Letters on the English and French nations; containing curious and useful observations on their constitutions natural and political*, London 1747, Ch. XXXVI, 207 (online). Bernard was director of the Bâtiments du Roi.

9 M. de Voltaire, *The temple of taste*, London, 1734 (British Library, Eighteenth Century Collections Online), 10, 20-23. French edition 1731, see: Voltaire, *Le Temple du Goût. Édition Critique par E. Carcassonne*. Lille 1953, 2nd edition. The text also reflects the French debate on taste during the ancien régime, see: R.G. Saisselin, *The Rule of Reason and the Ruses of the Heart. A Philosophical Dictionary of Classical French Criticism, Critics and Aesthetic Issues*, Cleveland/London 1970, 26-45 ('Beauty') and 192-202 ('Taste').

Fig. 5 *Haiku* of a *Crochet Table* (2001) with *The Killing of the Piggy Bank* vase (2009) from the Moooi collection

Fig. 6 *Skygarden*, 2007, Flos, aluminium, plaster

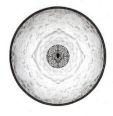

artfully reflect a woodland decor, and in which the bed appears to nestle in a woodland glade, she is in ecstasy.⁷

The language of the novella expresses an art de vivre of a world hovering between dream and reality. Wanders effortlessly translates this language of seduction into today's reality. He pens an ode to the luxury and theatricality of the history of applied art; his lamps, side tables and floral patterns, as well as his playing with reversal and asymmetry, are references to this. But Wanders places himself and his work in the now, imbues historical quotes with subtle irony, or packages them in banalities borrowed from real life. In the light of the banking crisis, we kill our old faithful piggy bank, transforming it into the lifeless *Killing of the Piggy Bank* vase. A small black head in the arabesque brain of the *Skygarden* lamp thinks beyond the boundaries of a plaster Rococo ceiling (fig. 8). His uncontrolled *Airborne Snotty Vase* resembles bone or rock but is in fact congealed slime from a sick video clip that will be recognisable to anyone familiar with Dutch autumns and winters (fig. 7, 8). Criticism of design is about the fear of decoration, imagination, illusion and seduction, precisely those elements that Wanders cherishes. People desire clarity, rationality and bounds. Anything other than this is considered frivolous, barbaric, or trendy. In the mid-eighteenth century, the time of *La Petite Maison*, the official tastemaker Jean Bernard wishes to restrict shapes to guard against extravagance. He finds nothing as difficult as exterminating bad taste – Chinese design, for example – declaring that an excess of opulence makes ornament 'foppish'.⁸ In 1734, the philosopher Voltaire defends his ideal Greek temple of good taste in *Le Temple du Goût*, while asserting that the Muslims destroyed that civilisation. He wishes for a back-to-the-temple movement with the power of 'Raison' and 'Verité'.⁹ But design is more than Reason, Truth, Facts and Function, and also richer than Western cultures. By revealing this, the work of Wanders has enormous topical relevance. His Refinement, Imagination and Seduction exist outside the blindness of the established history of design and testify to his power and singularity.

Fig. 7 *Airborne Snotty Vase Coryza*, 2001, Personal Editions, 3D printed polyamide

Fig. 8 **Still from *Airborne Snotty Vase* movie, 2001**

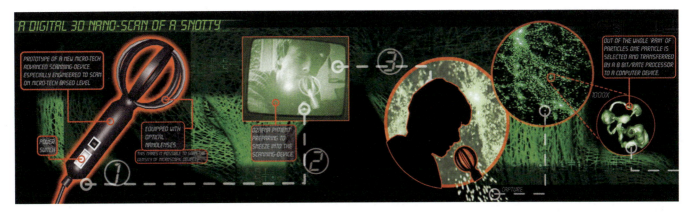

'A Completely Different Animal'

Interior Design by Marcel Wanders

Jennifer Hudson

Interiors affect our lives in immediate and very personal ways. Within our constructed world, more than any other design discipline, interior design has the power to define who we are as human beings. Whilst architecture is best appreciated and experienced visually from a distance, interiors enclose us, involve us, comfort and protect us. No matter the scale, they are intimate and have an inseparable link to our psyche. The men and women whose job it is to create our environments have the opportunity to manipulate our sentiments. As well as appealing to our conscious sense of aesthetics and physiological requirements, interiors can inspire and communicate. They speak to us subconsciously in their harnessing of memory, ritual, metaphor and association to engage us on both intellectual and intuitive levels. Yet the practice of designing interiors continues, above all, to be dominated by the need to deal with the physical and rational rather than the intangible and experiential.

In *Rethinking Design and Interiors*, Shashi Caan quotes the words of industrial designer J. Gordon Lippincott (1909-1989), the creator of the iconic Campbell's soup can, in his account of what qualities a well-rounded designer should possess. 'Art. [He] [sic] must understand and have an appreciation for the basic elements of visual design: colour, proportion, form, unity with variety, etc. He must have a cultural background in the arts of past eras, an appreciation of the history of art. He must have creative ideas... Of all basic qualities, the industrial designer must have art – without this, he is not a designer'. Caan goes on to update that portrayal. 'We would have to add that today's designer needs to have research skills, a strong global awareness of social and cultural issues, and a general knowledge of the latest technological, material and scientific advances'.[1]

1 Shashi Caan, *Rethinking Design and Interiors – Human Beings in the Built Environment*, London 2011.

'I had expected that interior design would be an addition to what I did, but that it would be more or less the same. I found out, however, that it is a completely different animal'

It is this balance – art and function; the poetic and the practical; the phenomenological and the physical – that informs the work of Marcel Wanders. Add to this the importance he places on collective memory and referencing the past, his sensitivity to cultural nuance, his creative imagination, as well as his innovative use of material and technology, and you begin to see why he is one of today's most interesting and intriguing designers.

Although Wanders started his professional life as a product designer, creating furniture and lighting that, ideas-led, spark the imagination and evoke individual memories and associations, interior design currently accounts for half of his studio's output. He first became interested in the field as a means of showcasing his

2 Interview conducted on 25 July 2013. Unless otherwise attributed, all further quotations are from this conversation.

3 Le Corbusier, *Vers une architecture*, Paris 1923. Translated by John Goodman as *Toward an Architecture*, Los Angeles 2007.

designs and to see if they worked within a situation that had been conceived specifically for their benefit, but soon began to appreciate the intellectual challenge that the added complexity of the discipline brought. He has often been quoted as saying that designing an object consists of one basic, strong concept that is formulated and brought to life in a very clean-cut way, whilst interiors are based on a thousand ideas that must all work together. He uses the analogy of a sculptor extracting layers from a piece of marble to reveal the beauty of the perfect form captured within, as opposed to a composer who adds density to an orchestral masterpiece. 'I quickly realised interior design was far more interesting than I thought. I had expected that it would be an addition to what I did but that it would be more or less the same. I found out, however, that it is a completely different animal. Interiors encompass people and they encompass time. It was creating space that caused me to grow because it has less foundation in modernism, and it matched my interests and passion to communicate and connect.'[2]

Designing interiors gives Wanders the opportunity to reach a large audience in a profound way. By addressing not only the functional (which Wanders considers to be the fundament for design, but nothing more) and logical, but also the subjective and subconscious relationship that the user has with his/her surroundings, he creates spaces that have impact and raise exciting questions about how interiors should or could look.

Behind all of Wanders' work is a defined yet open-minded design philosophy. 'I want to create a world that is more romantic, more humanistic, to take a step forward from modernism and realise that maybe modernism is done and we need a world that is more free-spirited and less technocratic; more respectful to the past and essential for the realisation of a sustainable future. Modernism discards the past every second, and so creates a throwaway society.' His contentious disdain for functionalism as anything other than an underlying necessity, and his attendant flamboyant and expressive style, is inseparable from the reservations he has about twentieth-century modernism and its machine-age aesthetic. He condemns the cold mantra of 'the house is a machine for living in'[3] and endeavours in his interiors to conceive more poetic and romantic spaces that are rooted in history and culture and filled with meaning and emotional content. His designs are people-oriented and not founded on the outdated doctrine of the Bauhaus which he believes reduced architectural theory to a formal criteria and rendered the user, for whom buildings are created, a lifeless abstraction, an almost non-essential participant in the design process. In the modern tradition, which looks only to the future, people are disconnected from their past and are alienated in an un-contextualised and anodyne setting. For Wanders, a modernist interior is a dead interior. Unlike product design, where a philosophical trajectory can be traced through various movements and styles, he sees no such academic discourse in the history of interior design. 'No real history of interior design has been written, and theoretical discussion is absent. The interior decorator sources and places objects within an interior and so pinpoints social codes, whilst the interior architect creates architectural clarity and an openness; an absence of interior. I work between these two disciplines to develop new dialogues.' He traces this lack of intellectual argument back to the Bauhaus. 'Le Corbusier drew his flats and his pillars and placed glass around them, and that was it (fig. 2). There was no philosophy about how to do an interior. In a way, the art of interior design does not exist.'

Perhaps as a reaction to Wanders' drastic departure from the clarity and simplicity of modernism's utopian visions, he has regularly been assessed in juxtaposition with minimalism, or as a postmodernist. It is an association he does not welcome. He considers that 90 per cent of designers do not even understand postmodernist ideology, and therefore have no idea of what it means to follow it. Such critique of Wanders' work misses the point that postmodernism, with its thrilling, multifaceted style that bears some parallel to Wanders, is based on a far-from-perfect future. Its atmosphere of irony, sense of societal fragmentation and decentred self is the antithesis to the humanistic, non-cynical and positive messages inherent in Wanders' work generally, but specifically in his interiors.

A more relevant argument could be made for an analogy between the essence of Wanders' interior design and the holistic aims of the Arts and Crafts movement in England in the second half of the nineteenth century. The group sought to reunite the relationship between designer, craftsperson and user that had been lost when the making of objects was transferred from human hands to machines. This separation of the physical, philosophical and psychological led to the obscuration of the human components of design. The movement advocated the reform of design at every level, and through every discipline, to turn the home into a work of art. By placing impor-

Fig. 1 **Le Corbusier, *Maison Dom-ino*, 1914. Plan FLC 19209 ©FLC/ARS 2014, courtesy Fondation Le Corbusier**

Fig. 2 **'Breathing' wall and mannequin in the Flagship Store of Mandarina Duck, London, 2002**

Fig. 3 **Design for seven Lute Suites and three meeting rooms in Ouderkerk aan de Amstel, 2005**

4 The VIP Room at the Hanover Expo 2000 showcases Wanders' early skill at maximizing the sensory elements of space; light, reflection and sound combine in hundreds of silver-coated objects hanging from the ceiling. In the Mandarina Duck Flagship Store in London a seven-metre yellow 'Gulliver', 40 breathing mannequins and a mirrored pillar that changes its surface from convex to concave in a constant fluid rhythm enliven an otherwise 'professional' shop design. Highly decorative, the Thor restaurant is nevertheless a straightforward and simple concept whose main purpose is to showcase Wanders' designs. It is entered from the lobby through an oversized version of his *Egg Vase*. The Blits restaurant is an early example of Wanders' use of performance and theatricality. Viewed from the river, it is conceptualised as a stage with the customers being the actors onstage.

5 The Westerhuis is home to Wanders' studio and Moooi's showroom, housed in a former school. There he has created a five-story complex for cultural entrepreneurs in central Amsterdam. The interiors blend floor and wall, and interior with furniture in a holistic wonderland of pattern, texture and surprise.

tance on handcraft, detail, patterning, material and surfaces they created interiors that connected to the user in a visceral way. 'Yes, I think you could say there is a relationship with the Arts and Crafts Movement as a non-linear, less rational doctrine which is more humanistic. It was the first such reaction to an industrial culture.'

Wanders employs many devices in his interiors to create the conditions required for space to be experienced intuitively. Mixing patterns and textures and alternating two- and three-dimensional surfaces, combined with changes in scale, shape and size, provide the indefinable stimulation necessary for our sense of well-being and comfort. He arranges space and objects in disparate yet meaningful compositions that provoke us to explore his world imaginatively and create un-envisioned and unanticipated journeys for ourselves. He provides experience through his use of theatricality and fairy-tale narrative, occasionally arousing us with his unexpected combinations of artefacts or phenomena, as well as mesmerising us with his boundless creativity. He draws on our collective memory by citing archetypes, using historical metaphors and adopting handcraft techniques, or working a craft aesthetic in a modern and innovative way, referencing our past in a contemporary idiom. The biggest gesture and the smallest detail are fused into a whole that is more than its constituent parts, and is difficult to sum up in purely visual or physical terms. His interiors are built for us. We, with our memories and desires, are their content. Their aim is to uplift the human spirit, share culture and entertain.

Wanders' interiors have developed with his understanding of the discipline and his growing intent, becoming ever more complex, ambitious and audacious. His early works, such as the VIP Room for the Hanover Expo 2000, the Mandarina Duck Flagship store in London (fig. 2), the Thor restaurant at the Hotel on Rivington (2004) and the Blits restaurant in Rotterdam (2005), although showing early evidence of some of the concepts outlined above, see him behaving like a product designer.[4] Essentially, he relies on a single idea that is then developed in a linear fashion. It is with the Lute Suites (fig. 3) that we begin to see a more gestalt approach to interior design. Here, Wanders wrought his personality over every inch of seven hotel apartments. Each is different, yet each completes an overall look with a strong visual rationale (fig. 4).

If the Lute Suites is where Wanders began to understand the intricacy of interior design, it is at the Mondrian South Beach Hotel in Miami (2008) where he started to put into practice what he had learned.

The Morgan Group's luxury hotel and apartments signifies a shift in direction.

In it we can see Wanders beginning to use fantasy and drama. A greater emphasis is placed on the use of archetypes and historical quotation together with the distortion of scale, the blurring of interior and exterior, the subtle use of site-specific citation, the referencing of craft techniques and the strong use of colour and patterning. We also see the introduction of what Ingeborg de Roode refers to as 'Unexpected Turn', namely, design elements whose purpose it is to make us look twice and realise that everything is not quite as it seems.

Space precludes an in-depth assessment of individual schemes, however, if we take examples from the Mondrian, we can see how Wanders adapts and repeats some of these techniques in later projects.

The concept behind the Mondrian is based on many narratives, the main one being the moment the Sleeping Beauty awakens to find herself in a world of wonder and opulence. In later projects Wanders puts less importance on specific quotation, adopting instead a collage of ideas wherein each space has its own significance. In the Andaz Hotel in Amsterdam (2012), for example, *Alice in Wonderland* is only hinted at. The dwarf-sized doors that line the passageway as we enter might make us feel we are falling down the rabbit hole, but they act more as a foil to the towering atrium with its constellation of stars and planets, which they precede, rather than allude to the story.

The use of symbols and citations from the past are omnipresent in all Wanders' interiors. In the Mondrian an instant of the two overlapping is evident in the giant bells – an ancient archetype for people gathering together – that are used inside and out in the arrival areas (fig. 5). Fitted with integral, baroque-style chandeliers they represent light and sound. Bells are used in many cases in his work, including the entrance hall to Westerhuis[5] (fig. 6), in the Andaz Amsterdam Prinsengracht Hotel

Fig. 4 **Seating area in one of the Lute Suites**

'Interiors encompass people and they encompass time. It was creating space that caused me to grow because it has less foundation in modernism, and it matched my interests and passion to communicate and connect'

and with crystal versions in the Hotel Kameha Grand in Bonn (2010).
Allusions to the past are found in objects, surfaces, patterning and in the adoption of ancient craft technique, and often overlap with quotations from other cultures and in site-specific references. In the Casa Son Vida in Majorca (2008), the subtle mix of old and new is visible through the entire villa; for instance, the classic profile of the curved walls contrasting with the newly custom-designed cupboards in straight yet traditional lines. Furthermore, in the jewel-like Residence in Amsterdam (2008) (fig. 7) surfaces are covered in highly ornate and rococo two- and three-dimensional

Fig. 5 **Bar at the Mondrian South Beach Hotel, Miami, 2008.**

6 The haiku is a Japanese visual poem. The essence of haiku is 'cutting' (kiru). This is often represented by the juxtaposition of two images or ideas with a 'cutting word' (kireji) between them; a kind of punctuation mark signalling the moment of separation and indicating the significance as to why the elements are related.

7 The Wunderkammer, or Cabinet of Curiosity, is an encyclopaedic collection of types of objects whose categorisation is beyond definition. They form a microcosm or theatre of the World and were particularly popular in Amsterdam in the seventeenth century when commercial shipping offered people the opportunity to collect exotic artefacts brought back by sailors from all corners of the globe. A particularly good example of Wanders' seeming to emulate this is in the shelves of objects on the wall of the Andaz atrium.

8 David Carlson wrote: 'Teapots in super size, huge Pinocchio dolls in mosaic, porcelain horse heads and knitted dogs. It was almost like to travel in a time capsule back to the glory days of Piero Fornasetti or the Memphis group and the postmodernism. Visiting the shows of Studio Job, Jaime Hayon and Marcel Wanders, among others, almost makes you feel as if visiting Alice in Wonderland or the wizard from Oz. Everyone seems to be part of the mass psychosis, the market is praising it, the press is writing about it and the consumers are gaping. It looks like a scene from the HC Andersen fairy tale, 'The Emperor's New Clothes'. An adequate question to highlight is if we should call it design, art or design-art, or if we have to invent a new category and word for these experiments. Some people call it neo-surrealism or expressionism-design, but we would prefer to refer to it as Vulgarism.' (davidreport.com/the-report/issue-7-2007-vulgarism.)

plasterwork. The blurring of exterior and interior is also evident in these two domestic interiors (as well as many others) through the use of organic motifs and artificial topiary and trees. The Villa Moda (fig. 8) is Wanders' most crafted interior. Based on the concept of the international souk, every monochromatic surface and detail is a reinterpretation of ancient Eastern patterns and was executed by a team of local craftsmen often reworking their age-old techniques in a modern way.

Playing with scale is a consistent element in Wanders' work, a method he uses to create surprise and emphasise the importance of detail. The idea of huge, sculptural pillars seen at the Mondrian is used again in Wanders' second hotel for Morgans, the Mondrian Doha in Qatar (due for completion in 2014); in this instance magnified in ever more complex configurations as they rise through each of the four floors. The casts for the original columns have been employed here as the base of the monumental lamps that line the lobby lounge (fig. 9). The 'Unexpected Turn' staircase, which intrigued us in Miami, is repeated in Doha but on a massive, awe-inspiring scale. Leading nowhere, it questions why things need to be functional.

Wanders places great importance on using non-literal local reference in his interiors. In Miami, Delft tiles in the apartment kitchens feature images of lifeguards, windsurfers and marlins. In Quasar (an apartment building in Istanbul due for completion in 2015), Wanders has enlivened what is normally a dead space, the lobby, with kinetic sculptures (fig. 10, 11). The giant head that greets you revolves slowly to alternately reveal an Asian and European face, signifying the importance the city has as a place where East and West meet. Lamps spin, transformed into Whirling Dervishes' skirts, whilst panels with paintings of tulips refer both to Marcel's Dutch nationality and to Turkey itself. Tulips were introduced to Holland from the East.

Fig. 6 **Entrance of the Westerhuis, Amsterdam, 2008**

At Andaz, references to Amsterdam and the Golden Age of the Dutch East India Company proliferate. The hotel was formerly a library, and Wanders has used images of seventeenth-century maps and pages taken from the antiquarian books belonging to the original archive as inspiration for the wallpaper and decor, referring to the city's nautical past and its having once been a centre of trade, shipping and cultural exchange. Another major theme within the overall design is the concept of haiku.[6] This type of visual poetry takes the form of seemingly incongruous juxtapositions of space and narrative to form unpredicted dialogues, as well as the unexpected placement of objects and artefacts that recaptures something of the eclectic spirit of the seventeenth-century fascination for the Wunderkammer[7]. In the Andaz, however, Wanders has taken it in a more provocative direction; what he refers to as connecting polarities. Two individual elements (a fish's head and a spoon, for example) are linked together to form a new and logical whole, symbolising Amsterdam's unique capacity to unite seeming opposites. In the city's coat of arms are found three X's, which Wanders has used as 'embroidery stitches' to fit things together and thereby unite them.

Fig. 7 **Part of the bedroom in Villa Amsterdam, a private house in Amsterdam, 2008, with a *New Antiques* armchair**

Critics of Wanders' work, especially his unrestrained and fantastical interiors, find his stylistic variety perplexing and sensationalist. Some even call it 'vulgar'.[8] Such censure does not appreciate the seriousness behind his creations, or the philosophy of humanism and connectivity that underlie them. Neither do they fully appreciate the important and vital role that fairy tales play, nor the necessity for fantasy,

Fig. 8 **Clothing store Villa Moda, Manama (BH), 2009**

imagination and drama as a palliative escape from personal and societal preoccupations.⁹ Pragmatically, fantasy also offers Wanders a means to create a theme, and allows the combining of elements that would not fit together in the real world.

Wanders does not work in isolation. Over the last couple of decades there has been a rise in popularity of the fantasy genre in all forms of media, from film and television to literature and fine art. Part of the current artistic climate is that of amazement. Marvel and theatricality offer the audience a chance to vicariously explore a wondrous world, as well as the human condition. Fantasy design and architecture has also inexorably risen in both popularity and critical recognition. Robert Thiemann quite rightly links the hotel designs of Andrée Putman (fig. 12) and Philippe Starck with those of Wanders.¹⁰ Both approach interiors not only as architects, but also as storytellers, film directors and artists. More recently, Spanish designer Jaime Hayon and Studio Job, a Dutch design duo, are also blurring the boundaries between art, theatre, decoration and design with surreal interiors full of inference and connotation that make us want to engage and participate, or stand back and question. (fig. 13)

Wanders is addicted to that moment when the last bit of an immense jigsaw puzzle falls easily into place. He describes working on an interior as initially being confronted by two boxes full of pieces: one full 'of my ideas, insights, goals and vision... materials I love, the colours I love; all those brilliant concepts, opportunities, possibilities and philosophies', and the other belonging to the client, brimming over with all of his/her (often conflicting) requirements, and with the special opportunities and challenges these inevitably bring. 'At first you throw them together and the mess is overwhelming. You have over a million pieces but the puzzle needs only a thousand. You look at the lids of the boxes for help but they are blank. And then you start to work. An endless game of trial and error, yet there comes that instant of realisation at the end when the very last piece seems almost to be sucked into the whole and everything is perfect.' It is a moment he describes as magical, and it is also what keeps him practicing in a field that has the power to frustrate him.

One of Wanders' key ideologies is that of durability. He uses historical metaphor in his product designs so that they will remain eternal. With the view that 'nothing ages as much as the new' he wants his work to be enduring: to be loved, cherished and never discarded. By their very nature, interiors are ephemeral. As our social mores change then so, too, must the spaces we inhabit. No matter how perfect the concept an interior designer may have, it is bound to be corrupted by the logistical and functional needs of the client, by the user, by financial constraint and by time itself. Wanders also has a strong conviction that design should always be positive. Its sole aim should be to make people's lives better. It should never carry a negative message or be cynical. At the time of going to print, Wanders is working on a series of twelve virtual interiors. These will always be exactly as Wanders envisages. Absent of people, the interiors speak only of themselves. They are magical and beautiful, but also hold a sense of foreboding and menace, allowing the viewer's imagination to make up its own stories of what has just occurred, or what is about to happen. Wanders' public persona is 'light, white, positive and friendly', which he says is not the complete picture. Like all of us, he has his darker side and moments of existential angst. The *Virtual Interiors* reveal more of his true nature; they contain a deeper repository of thoughts and emotions that he now desires to share.

9 Much has been written about the important role fairy tales play in articulating the human struggle to form and maintain a civilizing process. In his 1975 publication, *The Uses of Enchantment: The Meaning and Importance of Fairy Tales*, the Austria-born, American psychologist Bruno Bettleheim discusses the emotional and symbolic importance of fantasy in allowing the reader to grapple with their inner fears. Jack Zipes, retired Professor of German at the University of Minnesota, has lectured widely on the subject. In 1985 he published *Fairy Tales and the Art of Subversion: The Classical Genre for Children and the Process of Civilization*, which advocates fairy tales' political and social function in civilizing processes. More recently, British novelist and historian Marina Warner examines fairy tales themselves and the social and cultural contexts in which they were told to convey advice, warning and hope. 'The store of fairy tales, that blue chamber where stories lie waiting to be rediscovered, holds out the promise of just those creative enchantments, not only for its own characters caught in its own plotlines; it offers magical metamorphoses to the one who opens the door, who passes on what was found there, and to those who hear what the storyteller brings. The faculty of wonder, like curiosity can make things happen; it is time for wishful thinking to have its due.' (From *The Beast to the Blonde: Fairy Tales and Their Tellers*, London 1994).

10 Robert Thiemann, 'Staging spaces', *Interiors*, New York 2011, 5. 'Their affinity is particularly visible in their hotel designs. It is not a coincidence that both designers had their breakthrough at the Morgans Hotel Group: Starck with the Royalton, Paramount and Delano, and Wanders with the Mondrian South Beach Hotel. Both designers are in turn influenced by the groundbreaking work of Andrée Puttman for the Morgans hotel, an establishment that is part of the same hotel chain and is regarded as one of the first "boutique hotels". What is already visible in the work of Putman – the role of the designer as a film director – is amplified by Starck and Wanders.'

Fig. 9 **Design for Mondrian Doha Hotel, Doha, Qatar, completion expected 2014**

Fig. 10-11 **Design for lobby at the apartment building Quasar, and for the two sides of the rotating object, Istanbul, completion expected 2015**

His professional character, however, remains sanguine: 'If there's a single reason why design is so important to me, it is probably the potential it gives me to inspire, to contribute to the concept of the world changing in the direction my heart and head want to go. This is my primary focus as I work and play around in the garden of our industry... Design is a tool that allows us to reach out and inspire, to touch others and help makes lives magic and wonderful.'[11]

[11] Marcel Wanders, 'Grow more fish', foreword to the *International Design Yearbook* 20, London 2005, 6.

Fig. 12 **Andrée Putman, Morgans Hotel, 1984**

Fig. 13 **Studio Job, *Fountain I*, 2010, collection Groninger Museum, Groningen (NL), (permanent installation in Studio Job Lounge), polished and patinated bronze, glass, electrical components & pump, water, unique piece**

Marcel Wanders' Interiors in Context

Penny Sparke

In his short essay, 'Louis-Philippe or the Interior', the German cultural critic, Walter Benjamin, coined the evocative phrase, 'the phantasmagorias of the interior', to suggest that, in their inside, private, domesticated spaces, individuals foster illusions about their personal identities.[1] The psychological complexity of the interior recognised by Benjamin over half a century ago has continued to be a subject of much debate and discussion.[2] The fact that it has, of late, stimulated the emergence of countless popular magazines and television programmes about the interior indicates that the topic continues to fascinate many people. Marcel Wanders' forays into the creation of interior spaces, from the late 1990s until the present, are born of the same fascination. Making sense of his work in this field requires its contextualisation within the often contradictory phases of the evolution of the interior in the modern era.

Benjamin emphasises the fact that the interior is a modern phenomenon, born in the era of industrialisation and dependent on the separation between the private and public spheres. For him, it is represented by the mid-nineteenth-century, middle-class, and (to our contemporary eyes) over-cluttered parlour that supported individuals' 'phantasmagorias'. His metaphor of a compass enveloped in its soft velvet case evokes a sense of enclosure, dependency and tactility that he believes characterises the space of the interior.[3] In Benjamin's account, the interior's inhabitants are depicted as reflective, feeling individuals in search of their personal identities. In another metaphor, he compared the 'drawing room' to 'a box in a world theatre', thereby initiating a long-standing link between the interior and the theatre – whether that means the former being understood in terms of the human dramas enacted within it, or viewing the interior itself as a theatre from which an audience can look out at a world beyond.[4]

1 W. Benjamin, 'Louis Philippe or the Interior', reprinted in: C. Briganti and K. Mezei (eds.), *The Domestic Space Reader*, Toronto 2012, 103.

2 See, among others, C. Rice, *The Emergence of the Interior: Architecture, Modernity, Domesticity*, London 2006; V. Rosner, *Modernism and the Architecture of Private Life*, New York 2005; and P. Sparke, *The Modern Interior*, London 2008.

3 W. Benjamin, *The Arcades Project*, trans. H. Eiland and K. McLaughlin, Cambridge 1999, 220.

4 Benjamin op. cit. (note 1).

> **'I do study the rational quality and meaning, I do study the tactile and the emotional quality and meaning of things, to make sure that for everybody there's something inside that is meaningful and valuable (...).'**

Wanders is deeply aware of the theatrical possibilities of interiors. His Blits restaurant in Rotterdam, created in 2005, contains a series of stages and a row of curtains that frame the scene beyond them (figs. 1-3). Similarly, the sitting area adjacent to the pool in the grounds of his 2008 Mondrian South Beach Hotel in Miami is also framed by draped curtains, while the small cabanas located alongside resemble theatre boxes from which guests can observe the human dramas enacted before them (fig. 4). In the egg-shaped entrance to his 2003 restaurant interior on New York's Rivington Drive, Wanders employed another highly dramatic tactic, in this case one previously used by Frank Lloyd Wright in his Larkin Building (1906) and by John Portman in his Hyatt Regency Hotel in Atlanta (1967), that brings visitors through a dark, enclosed entrance into a light, open space of significant proportions.

Fig. 1 **'Blind date suite' in Blits**

Fig. 2 **Restaurant Blits, Rotterdam, 2005**

Although Benjamin is insistent that public inside spaces were rational places, devoid of the psychological complexity of the private spaces of the home, in reality, through the second half of the nineteenth century, the visual and material manifestations of the latter were transferred into the public, or semi-public, spaces of railway waiting rooms, hotel lobbies, theatre bars and department stores. The movement of the language of domesticity out of the home was intended to offer comfort to women who had to exit the domestic space in order to consume goods to then take back into it. The nineteenth-century parlour was therefore a highly gendered space, which, once removed from the home, acted as a strong stimulus for consumption. In that context, indeed, the interior arguably became an idealised concept to be ever aspired towards but never achieved. Its presence, in the second half of the nineteenth century in department stores and World's Fairs, bore witness to the high level of idealisation and commodification that accompanied its development. Its daily presence on our television screens plausibly reinforces its continued link with social aspiration.

In today's world, the boundaries between the private, domestic interior and the spaces of the public sphere – from workspaces to airports and shopping malls – are becoming increasingly porous. The ubiquitous potted plant is just one of the many emblems of nineteenth-century domesticity that still frame our daily lives across a wide range of indoor public spaces for shopping, travel and leisure.[5] A seamless integration of the private and the public characterises Wanders' interiors. His combination of the 'rational' (public) with the 'sensorial' (private), and of bare surfaces with highly decorated ones, represents a fusion of the two spheres and a recognition that each exists in the other. Striking juxtapositions can be found in many of his interiors, from the Blits restaurant in Rotterdam, where a simple wooden floor is combined with a large-scale rose mural, to his Thor restaurant, in which the white inner surfaces of its womb-like entrance contrast sharply with the textured walls and ceilings that contain it (see pp. 176 and 177). Several of his residential interiors combine plain walls with one that is covered with dramatically patterned wallpaper, while the large white tiles positioned around the outside pool of the designer's Mondrian South Beach Hotel are offset by an exuberantly patterned rug and floor cushions.

The association of the interior with women and consumption in the nineteenth century brought the concepts of the body, fashionable clothes and the indoor environment into close conjunction with each other. This new perspective on the interior underpinned the emergence of the interior decorator, the first professional to focus on the production of the discrete interior, who emerged largely as a result of visually skilled women taking over the task of decorating the homes of others who lacked the skills or taste to do it themselves. Elsie de Wolfe (1865-1950), for example, was an American pioneer in the field. Her background as an actress on the Broadway stage, on which she modelled couture gowns, and her subsequent transition from amateur to professional status as a decorator, starting with her own homes, meant that she prioritised the link between feminine identity and the interior. Her commitment to textiles (she was known as the 'Chintz Lady') enhanced her 'soft' approach to decoration, as did her use of historical styles, such as those from eighteenth-century France.[6] De Wolfe had little or no interest in the architectural shells that contained her interiors but focused, rather, on the formation of the identities of their inhabitants through the creation of stage sets. Given that she was working for a nouveau riche audience at a time of intense social mobility, the role of good taste as a marker of having arrived in society was all-important for De Wolfe. She worked within its constraints, recognising its power to change lives at that time.

[5] The author is currently working on a book entitled *The Jungle in the Parlour*, which will examine the role of plants in bringing domesticity into the public sphere from 1850 to the present.

[6] See P. Sparke, *Elsie de Wolfe: the Birth of Modern Interior Decoration*, New York 2005.

Fig. 3 **Wall with rose backdrop at the entrance of Blits**

Wanders' work mirrors many of De Wolfe's preoccupations. Like her, he uses historical styles, albeit with modern twists, and decoration plays a special role in his interiors. Working as he does in the early twenty-first century, however, Wanders has developed a hybrid idiom characterised by a fusion of the softness of textiles with the hardness of architecture (a legacy of his modernist education). Also, with the fragmentation of society that has occurred since De Wolfe's time, a recognised canon of good taste no longer has the same potency or meaning for Wanders and thus he works outside its constraints, preferring to let his ideas develop freely into the spaces, forms, colours and textures that emerge naturally from them.

The nineteenth-century perspective on the interior, documented by Benjamin and adhered to by interior decorators, who linked it to personal identity, taste, the fashionable (predominantly female) body, and theatricality, was seriously challenged and undermined in the middle years of the twentieth century by the (predominantly male) protagonists of the architectural and design movement known as 'modernism'. Attempts were made to ensure that the interior swung, pendulum-like, away from its earlier association with what was seen by its opponents as middle-class individualism, to become a mechanism for democratic change instead. In this process, the concept of rationality, as represented by the work of the machine, became highly valued. Modernism also embraced the nineteenth-century idea of the *Gesamtkunstwerk*, within which all aspects of a building were united under the dominance of architecture.

Wanders has little time for modernism, or for what he considers the limited language of design that represents the work of the machine. Nonetheless, he is committed, as were

Fig. 4 **Outside space Mondrian South Beach Hotel, Miami, 2008**

the modernists, to a blurring of the boundaries between architecture, interior design and furniture. Importantly, though, he refuses to accept the existence of a hierarchy among them. In spite of his clear allegiance to a postmodernist approach that references the past and utilises narratives, there remains a clear legacy of modernism within Wanders' work. His commitment to the hard architectural frame of his interiors (albeit softened by textiles, colour, texture and the dramatic effects of exaggerated scale) is ever present. In addition to his love of materiality, he also engages with the fundamentally modernist notion of space as a defining component of the interior, a concept that underpinned everything the early twentieth-century protagonists put into their buildings, from the fitted furniture that reinforced the importance of their interiors' architectural frames, to the skeletal, tubular steel furniture designs that, unlike their nineteenth-century upholstered antecedents, ensured that spatial flow was not disturbed. Wanders pushes the notion of space to its limits, however, and is keen to find new ways to define and articulate it. He talks of walls as the 'skins' of space and covers them with patterns that would have been anathema to the modernists. Space has thus become anthropomorphised in his interiors, which recognise the importance of the human body and their emotional impact on their inhabitants.

Through a combination of a renewal of Walter Benjamin's approach to the interior with a commitment to some aspects of the modernist project, Wanders' interior work can be understood as a microcosm of the history of the modern interior. It works across its dualities and resolves many of its contradictions. He has created spaces in which hard and soft are reunited, the theatrical and sensorial are merged with rationality, and the private and the public spheres are fused. In the process, however, the nineteenth-century concept of taste ceases to have any relevance and the modernists' hierarchical view of the world is forever banished.

'I'm Interested in You'

An Interview with Marcel Wanders

Robert Thiemann and Alexandra Onderwater

Fig. 1 **Marcel Wanders with his** *Rainbow Necklace* (2007)

The Westerhuis in Amsterdam is a Wanders Valhalla. Not only was Marcel Wanders partly responsible for the redevelopment of the five-storey former school building, it is also home to his design studio and the theatrically-styled showroom of design label Moooi, of which he is art director and co-owner.

From wall to wall, a mosaic in Wanders' famous ornamental patterning, covers the lobby floor. The entire building exudes the designer's presence, which comes into its own on the fourth floor. Monumental objects fill an ample conference room – all Wanders' designs, and from the Moooi collection. Black and white predominate.

We sit at an extensive table and sip water from the glasses Wanders designed for KLM Business Class.[1] Behind us, the immense *Skygarden* lamp (a design for Flos) competes with an equally striking but much smaller amorphous golden statuette in a cabinet. Above the long conference table, our eyes are drawn to Studio Job's gigantic *Paper Chandelier* from the Moooi collection. Here and there, Wanders' Personal

[1] This interview took place in Amsterdam, on August 21 and 28, 2013.

Editions are dotted about – many of which are large-scale, opulent designs created without a specific client in mind. Our immersion in Wanders' wondrous world is interrupted only by the view over the centre of Amsterdam. But knowing Wanders, as a creative figurehead of the city, it is an impingement he can live with.

Then Wanders walks in, impeccably dressed as always in a jet-black tailored suit, white shirt, colourful trainers and a necklace around his neck (fig. 1). The outfit that has become his uniform. Wanders himself says he may vary his signature look once every twelve days:

'I once spent a long time thinking about it. Now, I wear the same outfit every day. I like tasteful, distinct choices. It's who I am. This isn't a classic suit – the jacket is relatively short, the trousers wide-legged. You can play with clothing, suggest things. It is all design, of course. I don't understand why designers don't live their design potential. I apply it to aspects of my life. I don't see why not.'

You seem to make more of a business-like impression than a creative one. Is that what you want?
'I don't think that's true. On the contrary: I'm always recognised as creative, because of the combination of the suit, the necklace and the sneakers.'

Wanders lives his work. He puts his heart and soul into everything he makes, be it a sofa for Moooi, a make-up line for MAC, or a glass for KLM Business Class. And, whether you like them or not, you can tell, his designs go beyond pure functionality. They express a feeling, an emotion, a story.

'Embedding that subtle message in a consumer product is the fun of my work as a designer. Adding that extra touch is part of who I am and who I want to be. Going further than actually necessary. I may not try to make the best things, but to make things that are truly mine.'

You often put your logo, name or other kind of symbol, such as an image of your face with a clown nose, on your designs. What's the reason for that?
'If you work in the way I do, you need to sign your work, too. Support what you want to say. The logo stands for the studio, not me as a person. We chose black and white for the logo at quite an early stage – so it's less personal. It is a signature - nothing more, nothing less.'

Where did the clown nose come from?
'The logo is based on a photo that was once made for a magazine cover. I had designed a necklace for Chi Ha Paura...? (a Dutch jewellery brand). One of my few cynical pieces. And that image worked very well (fig. 2).

'To me, it's not a clown, more a court jester. In the classic sense – the only courtier allowed to tell jokes about the king because his loyalty is never in question. And that means he can hold up a mirror to the king, and let him see things he might not otherwise. I think it is wonderful: that you are licensed to be humorous because your loyalty is never in doubt.'

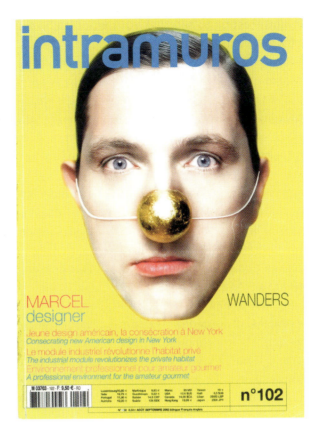

Fig. 2 **Magazine cover** *Intramuros* **with a portrait of Wanders wearing the** *Nosé* **wearable object on his nose, 2002**

'It is the reflection of the lightness in my work. And a token of loyalty to my public.' Wanders' first monograph was published in 1999. *Wanders Wonders* accompanied his exhibition at museum Het Kruithuis in 's-Hertogenbosch. The pocket-sized book presents ten perspectives on design. Among the things Wanders talks about is the 'baby face fixation', the disrespect for the old and an obsession with the new. He also talks about the sensory side of design, and being inspired by archetypes. Wanders illustrates his ideas by illustrating each statement with work – both his own, and that of others. 'The process of writing allowed me to translate my ideas and make them usable,' he says. 'It made them manageable, also for me.'

Did putting your ideas down on paper give you more control over them?
'Making the book gave me the tools to apply my perspective to design. I studied alternative therapies for a long time, such as NLP (Neurolinguistic Programming) and NEI (Neuro-Emotional Integration). Working with the subconscious. My girlfriend became ill; she developed cancer. For seven years, I lived in two worlds I was unable to unite. My passion for design and the classic Western world that it stems from, conflicting with the other, alternative, spiritual world. There was a distance between my work, and who I was.

'Then I turned 32, and I knew: this is a critical age. The first major work I made after this watershed was the *Knotted Chair*. And immediately I was outside, in the world.'

Fig. 3 *Urbanhike*, side table, 2013, Moooi, chromed steel, decalised aluminium wood transfer

It's interesting to see that your work is still guided by the insights you wrote down fifteen years ago.

'When my mother moved house, I came across my handwritten notes. Good God, I thought, was I working like this all those years ago? It makes you wonder whether you are always learning, or if, all along, you have been on the same path, and it is simply becoming clearer. I've given this a great deal of thought recently, working towards my 50th birthday. Naturally, ideas always become richer and deeper. But the themes that intrigued me then, are still at the heart of my work.'

Anyone musing on a secret success formula, a tried-and-tested way of working to attain a similar status, won't find any answers from Wanders. There is no success formula, he says. What's more, an interior project develops very differently from an object. An interior unfolds little by little, says Wanders. It is a result of a slow process of discussion, research, visiting the location and understanding the context. An object comes about in an entirely different way.

We are curious to learn how a recent design such as *Urbanhike*, comes into the world (fig. 3). How does Wanders begin with designing a side table with an old-fashioned walking stick as a handle, which was presented by Moooi in 2013 at the fair in Milan?

'First, I try to understand what we, as an organisation, want to achieve with Moooi. For 2013, we chose to present a complete interior, but had no interesting side table in our collection. So we decided to make a mobile object, a table with a handle. From there, the idea became bigger, because you make it urban. Mobility then has several facets. The first time I draw the design is for the team that will develop it to the final stage. But then, the basic design is already finished.'

So you sketch it for someone else?

'Designers' sketches are ideas about dimensions. They're caricatures. I use them to communicate what's in my head. Then begins a process of exchanging technical possibilities, and the design achieves an independent identity. The result may not be what I had in mind, which can be good or bad.'

However, many designs have a very different history of origin. They do not spring from a specific need but are an extension of other work. For years, Wanders has worked on families of objects that arise from a shared idea, and support each other in telling a bigger story. The context of a design – the family to which it belongs – contributes to its identity and logically colours our perception of it. Thanks to these over-arching themes, there is no need for Wanders to explain each individual design. This idea, in which the whole is more than the sum of its parts, enables him to develop a concept more rapidly.

'Think of *New Antiques* (fig. 4). But the studies of structure and now Delft blue, are these kinds of focal areas, a deepening interest over a longer period that results in an object with far greater resonance than one created as an isolated design.'

The designs of Wanders' early period – including the *Knotted Chair, Sponge Vase,* and *Egg Vase* – are mostly a quest for form. His work after 2005 demonstrates a different character. It is more expressive, personal and often more decorative. With *New Antiques*, has he discovered his form?

'*New Antiques* was a kind of discovery for me. In fact, so was using decoration in general. Because how do you do that – how do you deal with the baby face fixation? How do you make sure that objects truly share a relationship with life? How can you be rational without only being rational, and by doing so, capture people's imaginations? Decoration is a huge taboo in the design world. And breaking it is a gigantic achievement.'

Isn't decoration only taboo if it is purely an empty shell?
'Decoration is not even considered design. Despite a gradual shift taking place, the emotional and decorative are now tolerated, but only within certain limits.'
To Wanders, the entire discussion about the role of decoration in design misses the point. Decoration just is, he says. A designer can choose to use irrational aspects like emotion and surprise to add to a rational object which, claims Wanders, makes it easier for people to relate to it. Wanders says that his job is to strip decoration of its stigma.

'For Lute Suites (see pp. 106–107) I made a "good news" wall out of newspaper clippings (fig. 5). I was searching for a way to use decoration as an integral part of the design. I called the *Knotted Chair* a structure because referring to it as decorative was out of the question. At the time, I couldn't use those terms to describe it, even to myself.'

'The first time I actually called something decoration was when I was creating a pattern for porcelain flatware for Koninklijke Tichelaar Makkum (fig. 6). It was a liberating moment.'

Since then, the design world has followed his work with suspicion. Curators, professors and fellow designers talk about 'bad taste', 'design for the rich' and 'kitsch'. Wanders considers their criticism an expression of design fundamentalism, by people whose views are still firmly rooted in modernism.

'Modernism has deteriorated into a dogma that no one believes in; they simply borrow the stylistic elements.'

Fig. 4 *New Antiques*, 2005, Cappellini, wood, foam, leather, crystal glass

Fig. 5 **Design for *Goednieuwswand* in one of the meeting rooms in the Lute Suites in Ouderkerk aan de Amstel, 2005**

How does all this criticism affect you?
'I can see it for what it is. I love designing. I'm happy when an idea I have in my head, actually works. But the real reason I make things is very simple. I design to connect with the world. If possible, with the big world as well as the small, intimate world: my colleagues. In that sense, it's painful that I can't share my work with them in all its aspects.'

Does your work receive more criticism in the Netherlands?
'My work enjoys a more enthusiastic reception in other countries. The influence of modernism isn't as dominant there.'

Whether it's about fans or critics, Wanders' prodigious *oeuvre* is hard to place within the usual terminological categories. A modernist he certainly is not. Some see him as a post-modernist, a designer who quotes from the past to build a bridge to the future.

Would you agree with that?
'I think the world is already beyond post-modernism. I may not always be there, or not entirely, but my sensibility and desire certainly already are. It's just hard to pin down.'
How would you describe your oeuvre, then?

'As more holistic, romantic, humanist. Loving. I was trained as a modernist and my work is full of rationality. But it isn't only rational.

'The post-modern facet is evident in the fact that I free my work from modernist dogmas in general, and those of the future.

'Post-modernism is an anti-movement: my work certainly isn't. Post-modernism doesn't provide a solution for the problems facing us, and modernism is the enemy of those problems. What we need to do is the opposite of modernism, and independent of post-modernism; something entirely different – and that, I think, is what I'm looking for every day.'

If anything is a dogma in modernism, it is the truth, says Wanders. 'And the lie, that is the language of the designer. It is our poetry. We don't tell the truth: design is deception. No designer creates a product as ugly as it should be if it's meant to tell the truth. A plastic chair is made from oil, but what designer chooses to express that by making a greasy, dripping, black, toxic design?

'The only thing designers can do is attempt to give the lies a positive spin. White lies that aren't nurtured by cynicism.'

Doesn't purposeful lying display a lack of respect?
'Naturally I exaggerate. A designer makes things up. There is no truth, only a newly shaped reality. A proposition. A thought. An illusion. Even though it might be a wonderful story that makes everyone happy, we still aren't creating truth.'
'The lies I make are created from love. Take that candle (he points to a gold candle with a turned shape): there's an implication it's been made by hand, but everyone knows it's mass-produced. It's all about the illusion that is created. Why should a designer translate reality? There's so much more.'

Fig. 6 *Patchwork* plate, 2003, Koninklijke Tichelaar Makkum, painted and glazed ceramic

Rather than focusing on changing the shape of an archetype, his designs seem to add a skin that imparts a richness and tells a story. An observation Wanders partly agrees with. Although it applies neither to the recent *Carbon Balloon Chair* (fig. 7), nor many other designs. Wanders is especially struck by how, in essence, all his designs are always so simple and readable. 'The cartoon is always clear.' Wanders does not design inspired by his 'sense of form'.

'Where, then, is the context? Shape, structure, skin: they always emanate from a conceptual, rational framework. I seek the poetry between hard and architectonic on the one hand, and soft on the other. I make haikus that explore texture, colour and signs.'

For you, what is it ultimately all about?
'The collection of thoughts that interconnect and the choices on which they are based.' For him, beauty is found in relationships, the interplay of separate elements, says Wanders. This is a conclusion he reached while a student at the academy in Arnhem, when a watch design was dismissed as 'interesting, but too ugly for words'. Bemused, Wanders decided to study beauty. 'I laid down a grey blanket, and placed different objects on it. And I saw that beauty is all about relationships. I don't need to think up new shapes, I just have to place existing things in new relationships; there is nothing new, there are only new connections.'

Fig. 7 *Carbon Balloon Chair*, 2013, Personal Editions, carbon fibre, secured with epoxy resin

And what does that create?
'Something that respects everything that already exists.'

In that sense, you're not a 'shape-giver', as the Dutch word for designer, vormgever, literally translates.
'That's right, I'm a "shape-seeker". I love choosing from all the letters already in the world, rather than using new letters. That is the way I create new words.'

Earlier, you said that you design to connect with the world. How do you do that through a table or chair?
'You can't approach the objects I make purely through their physical presence. The story behind the design, the photography, the way the object is presented – thoughts, feelings, emotions. What really has meaning and content, is what you take away from it. In my work, art direction and communication also play a far greater role than they do in the practice of most designers. I realise that the physical aspect of a teacup is only a fraction of what I make – and often not the most important one. Everything you know about that cup affects the way you feel about it. *I am not interested in the material or form, I am interested in you.*'

What do you want your designs to mean to us?
'Design is about making make life better. More meaningful, beautiful, interesting. For me, design is not a place for expressing negativity, anxieties or frustrations but a place where I share beauty and love.

'I want people to love me. So I can create things that add to life's meaning. So I can feel safe, continue to grow, be independent.'

In other words, you give people something extraordinary, in exchange for which you want them to love you?
'I once sent an email to Magis: "I'll make you a heaven, can I be your star?" Something like that.' (Laughs.)

Marcel Wanders' Most Important Designs – a Selection

Ingeborg de Roode

Dipstick, prototype, dissolving coffee stick, 1986, Nescafé, instant coffee, plastic

Three *Dipstick* designs, various materials

Dipstick, 1986

Wanders first made a name for himself with designs such as *Dipstick*. Nestlé held a competition asking designers to create different coffee experiences for its Nescafé brand. Instead of taking the opportunity to design a new cup or another accessory, Wanders offered the product in an entirely new way: he created a little wand tipped with compressed Nescafé powder so the user can mix just the right amount of coffee and have a mixing stick at the same time.

Delft Blue, 2009

After Wanders designed *One Minute Delft Blue* (2006), a series of hand-painted objects, he returned to the same source of inspiration when designing a collection of accessories for his own label, Moooi. These vases, with their intriguing shapes (particularly the cylinder, which can be used both vertically and horizontally), are made by Royal Delft. It is an ingenious blend of a traditional method with modern shapes.

Delft Blue No. 4 (left and bottom), *No. 11* and *No. 1* (right), vases, 2008, Moooi, painted and glazed ceramic

Next page: Marcel Wanders and Erwin Olaf, publicity photo *Still Life* for the *Delft Blue Collection*, Mooi, 2008

Set Up Shades, floor lamp, 1989, cotton on a metal frame. This is the copy Renny Ramakers bought from the first series. Photo: Droog

Set Up Shades, 1989

This lighting design comprises a stack of lampshades – a simple, effective idea. The light came into being during a commission for telecom giant KPN. A couple of years later, it was the first product identified by Dutch design innovator Renny Ramakers as a new departure in design that ultimately led to the founding of the Dutch design company, Droog, and the huge success of Dutch design. Over time, Wanders would create a number of variations on this work, just as he's done with many of his other designs.

Marcel Wanders' Most Important Designs — Ingeborg de Roode

Richard Learoyd, *Can of Gold* project in London, 2003.

Can of Gold, vases from different editions, 2001–2012, Personal Editions, gilded sheet metal (above)
Can of Gold vases, 2001, during project in Budapest (2012), Personal Editions, gilded sheet metal (below)

Can of Gold, 2001

Wanders developed an idea for a gallery in Hamburg; the gallery director bought cans of soup and served the soup to the homeless. The empty soup cans were then gold-plated, and were sold for €250 each. The proceeds were given to the homeless in the vicinity of the gallery. Since 2001, Wanders' project has been staged in six cities in addition to Hamburg: Washington, D.C. (2002), Sydney (2003), London (2003), Mexico City (2006), Bruges (2007), and Budapest (2012). Photographer Richard Learoyd made a photo reportage of the London project. In total, the project raised around €350,000 for the homeless.

Prototypes from the series *Couleur Locale for Oranienbaum*, 1999, Droog: *Willow Chair* (top left), unpeeled willowshoot; *Disposable Cutlery* and *Bowl* (top right), poplar wood, duplex pressed; *Apple Juice Bottle / Birdhouse* (below right), ceramics

Drawing with *Willow Chair*, 1999

Products form the series *Couleur Locale for Oranienbaum*, 1999, Droog *Swing with the Plants* (top), wood, terracotta, rope, plant (later: polyethylene, polyamide rope), porcelain, sisal, steel; *Birdhouse*, wood (later recycled polypropylene), porcelain

Couleur Locale for Oranienbaum, 1999

Droog worked on a project in the East German town of Oranienbaum, the location of a palace that is home to a descendent of the House of Orange-Nassau. After the fall of the Berlin Wall, many attempts were made to rediscover and revitalize local skills and crafts. Droog's endeavour in Oranienbaum gave rise to many interesting designs but, due to a lack of funds for further development, none of the ideas were put into production. In the design magazine *Blueprint*, Gareth Williams dubbed the project 'design as PR', because the most important aspect of the project was its communicative value.

Card Case, card holder, 1994,
Marcel Wanders / Moooi, ABS, polypropylene
Commissioned by Stichting Kunst en Bedrijf

Card Case, 1994

Card Case was designed to hold eight credit cards along with similar cards. The patented closure mechanism enables the case to stay open or closed, as desired. It is one of Wanders' successful industrial products – among other things because this product lends itself perfectly to customisation, which makes it an ideal business gift. Until recently the *Card Case* was in production.

Breakfast of a Dwarf Rabbit, 1996

A carrot-shaped object hangs from a green cord. Wanders 'designed' this necklace in collaboration with his rabbit named Theodore. The part of the carrot Theodore ate was cast in plated silver. Since his training at the jewellery department at the academy of Maastricht, Wanders always has worked in this field.

Breakfast of a Dwarf Rabbit,
necklace, 1996, Wanders Wonders,
gilded silver, polyamide

Tape Necklace, 1996, Wanders Wonders / Personal Editions, tape with box of cardboard

Tape Necklace, 1996

The *Tape Necklace* is related to *Breakfast of a Dwarf Rabbit*, as it contains a recording of the sound of a rabbit munching on a carrot.

Big Shadow Special: Eyeshadow, floor lamp, 2011, Cappellini, metal, ink jet printed pvc and viscose fabric

Art print with *Big Shadow* lamps, 1998, Cappellini, 2012. Art direction: Marcel Wander

Big Shadow, 1998

The *Big Shadow* is a design that unites Wanders' playfulness with scale and interest in archetypes. The *Wax* model of 1992 was a harbinger of this design. The *Big Shadow* lamps certainly live up to their name (the largest is 202 cm high). Originally, these lamps were produced only in white (see p. 172), but other variants have since appeared, including a plastic version in red and the *Eyeshadow*, a version with the *Eyes of Strangers* pattern (2011).

Detail *Sponge Vase*

Sponge Vase, 1997

In 1997, the porcelain manufacturer Rosenthal invited Droog to come and work at their factory. Wanders sought a method to capture the fragile qualities of porcelain. A mould wouldn't work because the porcelain object would be a cast of the mould and would lack detail, so Wanders developed a production process without a mould: he dipped natural sponges into porcelain clay and fired them in the oven. The sponge was burned away to reveal an incredibly delicate texture. With this technique, every vase is different. Wanders also used this method with industrial foam.

Sponge Vase, 1997, Droog For Rosenthal / Moooi, glazed porcelain

Presentation of *The Wanders Collection Soapbath Series* with, among other things a *Monster Chair* and *Can Can*-lamps, 2005-2011

Soap Stars from *The Wanders Collection Soapbath Series*, soap, 2005, Bisazza

The Wanders Collection, Soapbath Series, bathtub and sink, 2005 / 2011. Bisazza, fibreglass, against a wall of Bisazza mosaïcs

Soapbath Series, 2005

The title *Soapbath* refers to the shape of the bath (and wash basins) and is based on the shape of a typical bar of soap. To promote the design, real soaps were made in the shape of the bath and handed out as promotional gifts during the design's introduction in Milan. It is an excellent example of playing with scale – a game at which Wanders excels.

Sparkling Chair, 2010

'Mankind will find its future floating on the breath of little children.' Wanders uses this statement when referring to his *Sparkling Chair* to emphasise the fact that the firmness of the construction relies on the air in the various components. The chair, inspired by a PET bottle of carbonated water, was initially made using a blow moulding process, which allows its plastic skin to be extremely thin. Later, manufacturer Magis decided not to use compressed air, which resulted in a thicker skin. For this reason, the current Magis version was given a different title, *Still*, and is not sold under Wanders' name.

Sparkling Chair, 2010, Magis, blow-moulded polystyrene

Marcel Wanders' Most Important Designs — Ingeborg de Roode

Print, sofa, 2005, Moroso, wood, polyurethane and polyester fibre with *Flying Table* (2005) for Moroso

Schematic display of the different pattern sections for *Print*

Print, 2005

This sofa, with its ingeniously printed fabric, is the first design that Wanders made for Moroso. Although it may not immediately be noticeable, the fabric is specially printed so that the pattern flows continuously and hides the seams. A *Print* pouffe was added in 2005.

Kameha Grand Bonn Hotel, 2010

A corporate hotel in Bonn designed as a boutique hotel. Wanders used large patterns in the hall on both the floor and walls. The larger-than-life-sized scale reappears in other elements as well, such as the lights in the shape of gigantic bells, and the huge flowerpots in which saplings grow.

Hall Kameha Grand Bonn Hotel, Concept & Art Direction: Marcel Wanders, Bonn, 2010

Publicity photos for *Couture: Henry* with, among other things, *Haiku* plates (2005–2007) for B&B Italia (left); and *Stella* with, among other things, a *Crochet Chair* (2006) and *Crochet Courage* (2007) (right); wallpaper, 2008, Graham & Brown, printed paper. Art direction: Marcel Wanders

Couture, 2008

This wallpaper collection comprises a number of designs ranging from geometric, crystalline-type motifs to more baroque-inspired patterns. The photographs for the publicity campaign depict people in impossible positions. For the photo shoot, Wanders had special rooms built which could be tilted by 45 or 90 degrees, skewing reality.

Zeppelin, hanging lamp, 2005, Flos, cocoon, crystal, perspex, steel

Zeppelin, 2005

Flos asked Wanders if he'd like to use the cocoon technique, a method that was used in the 1960s by Achille Castiglioni. Castiglioni is one of Wanders' most admired designers, and Wanders describes him as having given shape to 'untouchable lightness'. This hanging lamp clearly reveals Wanders' interest in existing shapes: inside the cocoon is a traditional chandelier with flame light bulbs.

New Antiques, seating and tables, 2005, Cappellini, wood, foam, leather, crystal glass

New Antiques, 2005

This furniture series for Cappellini is made using traditional wood-turning techniques. According to Wanders, the manufacturer was refused participation in the prestigious Design Biennale Interior Kortrijk because of the introduction of this series. This is a telling example of the design fundamentalism that Wanders says holds sway in the design world. To mark the introduction of the series, Wanders published his manifesto *War on Design!*

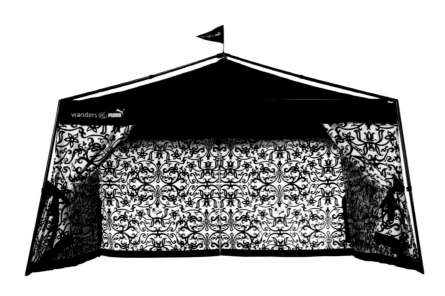

The Villa from the *Marcel Wanders By Puma Collection*, tent, 2006, Puma, aluminium, printed polyester

The Villa, 2006

'I hate camping...but I love lounging in style'. The gazebo-style lounge tent, the structure of which also functions as a camera tripod, exudes urban style and luxury and certainly has very little in common with what camping is usually thought to be. Wanders continued this urban look in his collection, designing a trolley that can also serve as an ice box to chill champagne and fruit salads.

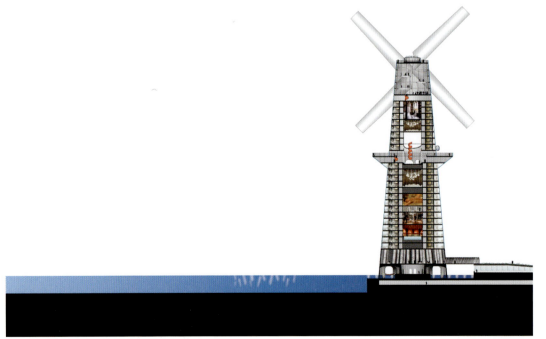

Molen op de Kop (Windmill on the north), design for a landmark in the shape of a windmill for Java-island, Amsterdam, 2011

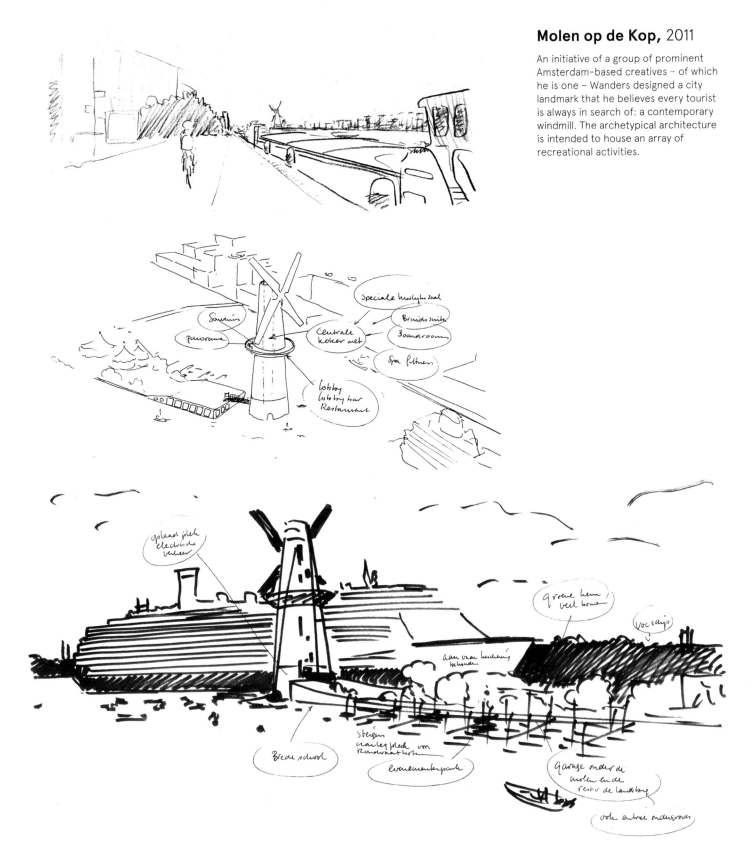

Molen op de Kop, 2011

An initiative of a group of prominent Amsterdam-based creatives – of which he is one – Wanders designed a city landmark that he believes every tourist is always in search of: a contemporary windmill. The archetypical architecture is intended to house an array of recreational activities.

Airborne Snotty Vases, 2001

Wanders took images of airborne mucus sneezed by people suffering from five different ailments, scanned them, magnified them a thousand times, and had them 3D printed as hollow shapes with an opening at the top to create a vase. In this design, Wanders capitalized on the potential of 3D printing to produce supposedly 'impossible' shapes. In addition to the white variant, the design is available in several other versions: black, gilded, and with the brightly coloured Interpolis pattern (see p. 110). Wanders won the WIRED Technology Award for this innovative project.

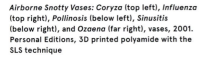

Airborne Snotty Vases: Coryza (top left), *Influenza* (top right), *Pollinosis* (below left), *Sinusitis* (below right), and *Ozaena* (far right), vases, 2001. Personal Editions, 3D printed polyamide with the SLS technique

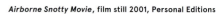

Airborne Snotty Movie, film still 2001, Personal Editions

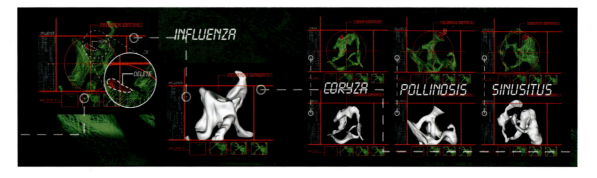

Tattoo, 2013

Wanders designed a tattoo for pianist Iris Hond's hands and forearms. The tattoo will probably be done shortly. The interest of Wanders for 'skin' is literally translated here.

Test with the design for the tattoo for Iris Hond, with (from left to right) Wilma Plaisier, Marcel Wanders, Iris Hond

Designs for tattoo for pianist Iris Hond, 2012–2013, painted and glazed ceramic

Designs for *Monster Chair*

Monster Chair, 2010, Moooi, steel, synthetic leather

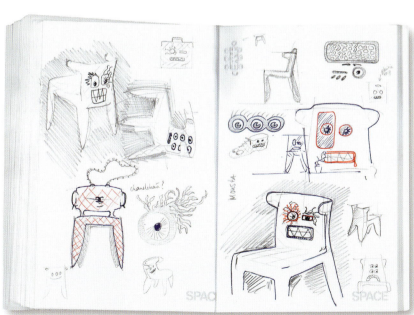

Design sketches for *Monster Chair*

Monster Chair, 2010

The monster that is embroidered onto the back of the chair has stepped out of Wanders' dreams. It is an expression of the designer's darker side, although the story he wrote about it on his website also mentions seven muses who he hopes to meet after his death, which gives the tale an upbeat ending (see www.marcelwanders.com/products/seating/monster-chair/). To date, only one of the sketches for the embroidered designs has been produced.

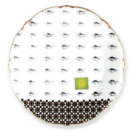

Patchwork, 2003

Wanders chose five types of plates from the porcelain manufacturer Tichelaar's traditional collection and designed 30 different decorations (six for each type). Each plate is partly transfer printed and partly hand-painted. The combination of all these different decorations creates a delightfully diverse dinner service. This project, Wanders claims, was the first time he was able to work without the constraints of the 'modernist dogma', casting inhibitions aside to transform a product with exuberant motifs.

Patchwork, from left to right breakfast plates, soup plates, underplates, main course plates, side plates, 2003, Koninklijke Tichelaar Makkum, painted and glazed ceramics

One Minute Delft Blue, 2006

For Royal Delft, a manufacturer of delftware, Wanders painted traditional items such as figurines, vases, and plates, in just one minute. He transformed mass-produced objects into unique pieces with a modern, quirky look derived from his unorthodox way of painting. He first used the *One Minute* concept in 2004 for sculptural objects made from clay.

One Minute Delft Blue, vases (above) and tulip vase (right), 2006, Personal Editions, painted and glazed ceramic

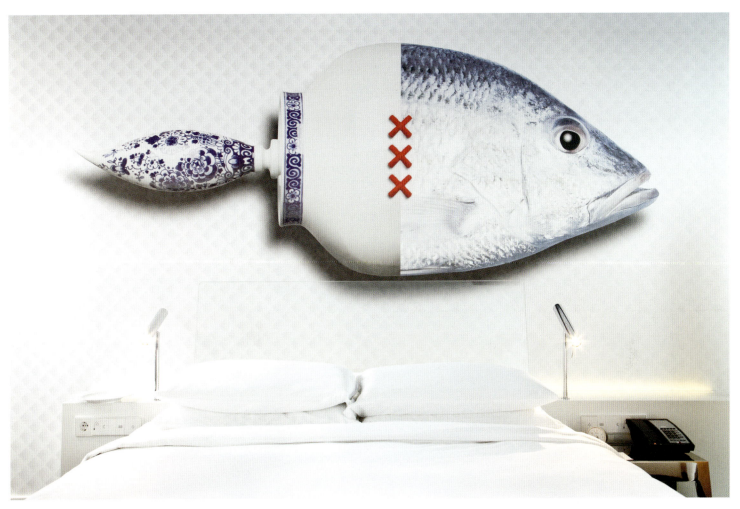

Lobby and room at the Andaz Hotel, Amsterdam, 2012

Andaz Amsterdam Prinsengracht Hotel, 2012

This hotel is situated in Amsterdam's former public library, which inspired many of the features of its interior design, such as old maps and illustrations from books about the city. References to delftware are also very much in evidence. The prince who is situated in the garden 'screams' your lost dreams to you soundlessly.

Restaurant, *Prince* in the garden, Delft Blue Room and meeting room at the Andaz Hotel, Amsterdam, 2012

Tulips, 1992

When Wanders was part of the design studio WAAC's, the collective designed new snacks. The refreshments were to be a healthy alternative to French fries. Wanders came up with *Tulips*, a tasty rice-and-herb finger food. The idea was that people could bake the *Tulips* in an oven, and in three minutes the little tulip-shaped snacks would 'blossom' in their cardboard packaging.

Marcel Wanders for WAAC's, *Tulips*, snacks, 1992, rice, herbs (model made of polyurethane foam)

Couple, vase, 1990. Koninklijke Tichelaar Makkum, glazed ceramic, sand-lime brick, beech, copper

Couple, 1990

This vase is an early example of a design in which dialogue is a key aspect, one that conjoins old (the traditional vases) and new or unusual (the sand-lime bricks). The object was designed for the exhibition 'Nederlandse Beeldende Kunst Textiel' in 1990 in Gallery Het Kapelhuis in Amersfoort.

Skygarden, 2007

Wanders explains that the *Skygarden* lamp was inspired by his moving house, when he missed the magnificently decorated ceiling rosette from his former home. By designing the *Skygarden*, he was able to take it with him. The interior of the hanging lamp is made entirely from plaster, a most unusual material. The design only reveals its secret when you look up and see the inside of the lampshade.

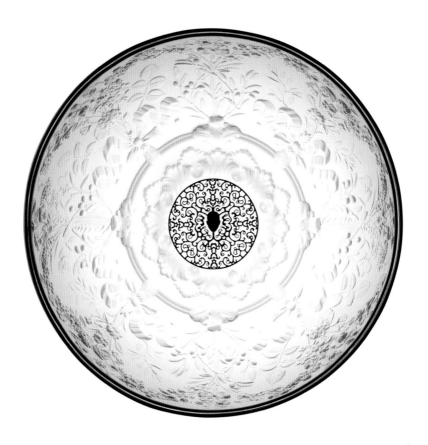

Skygarden, hanging lamp, 2007,
Flos, aluminium, plaster

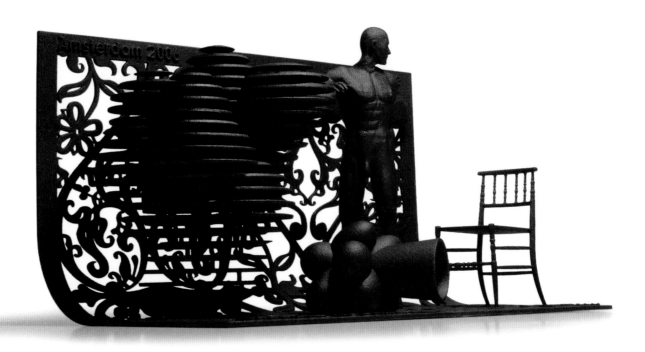

3D Haiku Uova Scure, 2006, Personal Editions, polyamide, 3D printed with the SLS technique

3D Haikus, 2006

In 2006, Wanders made four still lifes from 3D printed polyamide in which he included miniatures of his own designs. He designed a new series in 2013.

Stone Chair, lounge chair, 2001, Cappellini / Personal Editions, polyester, covered with silicone and pebbles

Stone Chair, 2001

The Stone Chair beautifully illustrates Wanders' interest in the skin of objects. He uses pebbles to give the chair an extraordinarily tactile, three-dimensional surface.

Lute Suites, boutique hotel, Ouderkerk aan de Amstel, 2005, room with amongst other designs *Coffee Table* (2004) for Bisazza (left page), bathroom with *Pipe* shower for Boffi (2000) and Bisazza mosaics (far left), laser cut steel 'parquet' floor (left), design for one of the suites (right), bathroom with digital printed tiles and *Soapbath* for Bisazza (2005, bottom)

Lute Suites, 2005

This hotel in Ouderkerk aan de Amstel consists of ten cottages, of which seven were uniquely designed as separate luxury suites. Eye-catching features include laser-cut 'parquet' floors in two colours (zinc-coated and blue-stained), Bisazza mosaic walls and other wall finishes such as digitally printed tile, and the 'good news' wall (see p. 61), which features newspaper clippings with nothing but heart-warming articles.

Murano Bags, handbag, knapsack and shoulder bag (there are also a wallet and a wristbag), 2001, Mandarina Duck, sandwich of polyester foam and textile, metal

Murano Bags, 2001

Wanders had the idea for these bags when he woke one morning to find his face creased. He interpreted the creases as signs of wisdom, age, and experience. The spherical shapes, creased here and there, were created by inflating a piece of foam sandwiched between two layers of fabric (hence the valve), and then allowing the inflated shape to cool. Wanders was inspired by Murano glassblowers for this industrial technique, which is used to create unique objects; no two *Murano* bags are exactly alike.

Aqua Jewels at 'Swarovski Crystal Palace' presentation in Milan, crystal shower and crystal mosaic wall, 2008, Swarovski and Bisazza, chromed brass, Swarovski crystals, Bisazza crystal mosaic

Design for 'Swarovski Crystal Palace'-presentation in Milan, 2008

Aqua Jewels, crystal mosaic elements, 2008, Swarovski and Bisazza

Swarovski Crystal Palace, 2008

For Swarovski's spectacular 'Crystal Palace' exhibition project in Milan, Wanders not only designed a chandelier with an integrated shower head, he also developed tiny cut-crystal tiles for glass mosaic company Bisazza and crystal manufacturer Swarovski, and applied Swarovski tiles in a monumental wall decoration – Wanders often gives a project a little extra edge.

Stonehouses, flex office space, 2002, commissioned by Interpolis, Tilburg (NL)

Stonehouses model, Interpolis, 2002

Stonehouses, 2002

Numerous designers teamed up to create one of Holland's most experimental co-working office environments at the Interpolis Headquarters in Tilburg. Wanders designed a kind of park as a place for the staff of Dutch insurance company Interpolis to meet. The dark brown *Stonehouses*, one of which is decorated with a cheery floral motif, are among Wanders' first designs to highlight decoration. He later used the pattern several times in different designs.

Marcel Wanders' Most Important Designs · Ingeborg de Roode

Lucy, candlestick, 1999, Goods, injection moulded metal

Lucy, 1999

A candlestick with an innovative construction technique: five identical parts are held together by a screw inserted below the foot.

Wattcher, energy meter, 2009, Innovaders, ABS, rubber

Wattcher, 2009

The *Wattcher* is a device to help monitor electricity consumption. Wanders created a seemingly simple product from materials that give it a tactile appeal, which makes it more than simply a practical accessory. He also designed an educational program for families, encouraging them to compete with each other to see who can use the least electricity – 'The Battle for Watt'.

Bottoni, 2002

With *Bottoni,* Wanders designed an easily adaptable sofa. The collection included a range of covers that could be attached to the sofa back with buttons, allowing consumers to experiment with a number of different looks.

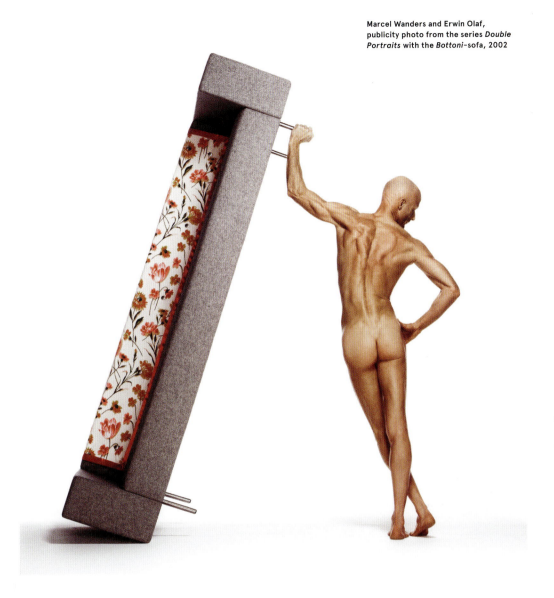

Marcel Wanders and Erwin Olaf, publicity photo from the series *Double Portraits* with the *Bottoni*-sofa, 2002

Bottoni, sofa, 2002, Moooi, multiple density foam, plywood, stainless steel

SLS Vase, 1999

Wanders made a 3D printed vase for the project 'Vase for the Occasion', in which designers created a promotional gift for different towns in the Dutch region of Brabant. 3D printing utilises laser beams to create any conceivable shape from polyamide granules. Wanders exploited the technique to the fullest. Until then, 3D printing had been used only to produce prototypes and models. Wanders is the first designer known to have used 3D printing to create a reproducible end product. Because Eindhoven finally chose a different design, only one copy was ever made.

SLS vase, vase for the Municipality of Eindhoven for the project *Vaas voor de Gelegenheid* (Vase for the Occasion), 1999, polyamide, 3D printed with the SLS technique

Art print *Wanderduck*, Flagship Store for Mandarina Duck, London, 2002

Wanderduck, Flagship Store for Mandarina Duck, London, 2002

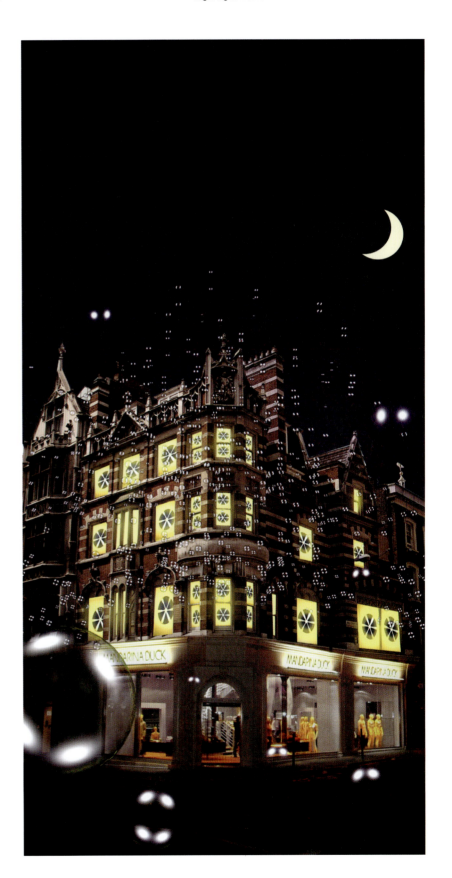

Wanderduck, 2002

The flagship store of the Italian luggage brand Mandarina Duck received a very human face through Wanders' interior design. Invited to bring the store to life, Wanders created unique mannequins that 'breathe', as well as a 'breathing' wall of stretched plastic membrane behind the store's staircases. Gulliver, one of Britain's most famous travelers, towers in the centre of the space at seven metres tall, and integrates a sound system. Passers-by saw slowly rotating fans in the window display, and a steady flow of bubbles rising up from the store's basement.

Serie apparaten, v.l.n.r. van boven naar beneden:
Carrie USB-stick; *Domino* luidsprekersysteem;
Merlin USB-audiosysteem transmitter; *Pandora*
multimediasysteem; *Egg* luidspreker; *Mathilda*
draadloze transmitter; *Theatre* multimediasysteem;
Wave-TV magnetron met tft-scherm en ingebouwde
dvd-speler, 2006, HE, verschillende materialen

Electrical appliances for HE, 2006

The Dutch company HE (formerly known as Holland Electro) commissioned Wanders to design a series of electrical devices. Wanders proposed a number of innovative products, such as a microwave with a TV in the door, and a USB stick that can send a signal from a laptop straight to wireless speakers. It is an interesting mixture of Wanders' personal, humanist design, and product typologies that are generally associated with 'hard industrial design'. Unfortunately, the products were soon withdrawn from the market due to technical problems.

The Knotted Chair

Ingeborg de Roode

[1] On the application of new materials and techniques and their impact on furniture design: Ingeborg de Roode, 'Form follows function? 150 years of furniture design', in: *Stedelijk Collection Reflections*, Rotterdam/Amsterdam 2012, 313-332.

[2] Eurocarbon still manufactures the carbon-aramid filament exclusively for the *Knotted Chair*. Conversation between the author and Arnold Voskamp of Eurocarbon, 27 May 2013.

Marcel Wanders' international breakthrough came in 1996, when his *Knotted Chair* was presented in Milan. The chair – which unites many, sometimes conflicting, qualities (traditional, innovative, soft, hard, handcrafted, industrially-produced, low-tech, high-tech) came into being during the first project initiated by Droog Design 'Dry Tech'. In collaboration with the aerospace engineering faculty at Delft University of Technology, designers Marcel Wanders, Hella Jongerius and Martijn Hogendijk were invited to combine the ultra-light materials in which Professor Adriaan Beukers and his team had specialised, with methods of traditional craft. This was one of many occasions in design history when designers seeking inspiration for innovative (furniture) designs turned to the aviation industry, just as Alvar Aalto and Charles & Ray Eames had done in the past.[1] New materials or techniques are rarely developed specifically for the furniture industry, one of the exceptions being the nineteenth-century woodworking technique of using steam to bend solid wood. Both Wanders and Jongerius received funding for their research from the Netherlands Foundation for Visual Arts, Design and Architecture and began experimenting with a design in which they intended to apply the materials as textile (p. 122). At Delft University of Technology, researchers largely produced composites in flat sections, an entirely logical form given their application in the aviation industry. Jongerius chose to weave a lamp from fibreglass, which was partly hardened with epoxy and Wanders experimented with carbon filament.

During attempts to use carbon cord to hand-knot a chair, Wanders discovered that it easily breaks. Wanders asked Eurocarbon in Sittard, which manufactured the material, to help find a solution. The most obvious solution was to encase the carbon filament in a different material. After experiments with fibreglass, Wanders returned to carbon which, weight-for-weight, is ten times stronger than steel. They eventually arrived at a woven aramid cord around a carbon fibre core, a strong and light material primarily used for bulletproof vests, cables, firefighters' uniforms and composites for the aviation industry.[2]

Knotted Chair, lounge chair, design 1995-1996, made in 1997, Droog, Cappellini and Personal Editions, knotted aramide fibre cord with carbon core, secured with epoxy resin, sand blasted

Image from the series of 9 photographs made for publicity purposes, 1996–1997, Wanders Wonders.

3 For example in: Lucia van der Post, 'A Wanders Full World', *Financial Times*, 6 February 2010.

4 Many recent publications state that the chair is dried upside down over a mould, but that is incorrect. I haven't been able to find the source of this misunderstanding, but it most probably originates from Gaudí's upside-down shapes.

5 'Gaudí revisited'. To the best of our knowledge, this connection was first made, in: exh. cat. *Industrieel Ontwerpen*, catalogue of the Rotterdam Design Prize 1997, Rotterdam 1997, cat. nr. 179, see http://designprijs.nl/archief/1997/97/15.html

6 Conversation between the author and Wanders, 2 September 2013.

7 Tijs van den Boomen, 'Hightech-macramé', *Intermediair*, 13 March 1997, 37.

Wanders chose the traditional technique of macramé, a method with a decidedly frumpish image, often associated with hanging plant-holders and bags from the 1970s (p. 123). He cultivated his interest in the technique retrospectively with the comment that he had loved handcrafting when it was out of fashion, and had been forced to hide books on the technique behind his porn magazines.[3] Wanders has the habit of coupling outspoken comments with designs and using them in (almost) every interview, thereby creating a kind of mantra for his work.

Four bundles of cords form the legs of Wanders' design. The chair is then immersed in epoxy and allowed to dry hanging, which hardens it and creates a kind of invisible construction.[4] This is followed by sandblasting the object, which restores the textile character of the cord. The black carbon filament is only visible at the ends, where the cords are cut after hardening (p. 123).

During the hardening process the chair is hung from four points (two at the top of the back support and two at the front, on the edge of the seat (p. 123) creating a natural curve that both forms the seat and back. Parallels were soon drawn between the design technique of Catalan architect Antoni Gaudí who worked with hanging chain models and applied these shapes, in reverse, in his buildings such as the Sagrada Família in Barcelona.[5]

For a much faster and more industrial process, Adriaan Beukers suggested that Wanders could place the aramid cord with a carbon fibre core randomly in a mould, and harden it using epoxy. But Wanders declined, preferring the craft production method without a mould.[6] After all, a mould always creates a sharp edge, Wanders feels.[7] He believes that the slight variations created by hand-knotting the cord give people the feeling that they have a unique object in their home. 'I wanted to make a product that doesn't look industrial, a design that shows that it is lovingly made especially for someone, with the same kind of aura as an old worn-down wooden cupboard. Knotting is a technique with which you can achieve this artisan atmosphere.'[8] Besides the imperfect, handcrafted and humanist (non-technological) factors, the decorative aspect of the knotting was paramount for Wanders.[9] The design proved to be a miracle of transparency – so delicate that at first many wondered if it was suitable for use. Wanders made a series of photographs showing beyond any doubt that the design was sturdy enough to stand on, even if the person in the photographs is a little girl who has taken care to first remove her shoes before climbing onto the chair to reach something. The fragile construction weighs a mere 1.4 kilos, which is incredibly light for a lounge chair.[10] You can pick it up with your little finger. The design exemplifies a fascinating marriage of high-tech (the material) and low-tech (the production method and the reference to a classic Egyptian type of chair).[11] This combination was particularly prevalent in the Netherlands in the 1990s.[12]

The chair proved to be the right design at the right time, and immediately attracted enormous attention following its presentation in Milan. It was one of the first examples of traditional craft to receive a contemporary, quirky reinterpretation. A journalist for the Italian magazine *Interni* even referred to the object as the 'only interesting' design during the entire fair.[13] In the catalogue for the Rotterdam

8 'Ik wilde een product maken dat er niet industrieel uitziet, een ontwerp dat laat zien dat het met liefde speciaal voor iemand gemaakt is, met dezelfde uitstraling als een oude versleten kast. Knopen is een techniek waarmee je die ambachtelijke atmosfeer kunt bereiken.' Marieke van Zalingen, 'Breien en knopen met high-tech vezels', *Eigen Huis & Interieur*, 29 (1996) 11, 12-13, quote on 13.

9 Conversation between Wanders and the author, 16 May 2013. Renny Ramakers also referred to the decorative aspect that can be an intrinsic part of a design. By way of example, she cited (among others) the *85 bulbs light* by Rody Graumans and the stitching in the felt hand basin by Dick van Hoff. Renny Ramakers, *Droog Design. Spirit of the Nineties*, Rotterdam 1997, 61.

10 For a long time, one of the lightest chairs was the *LightLight* (1987) by Alberto Meda, made from a woven carbon skin with a Nomex honeycomb core that weighs around 1 kilo. In 2013, Wanders made a chair from hollow carbon tubing that is only 800 grams (see pp. 162-167). Although he claims that such designers' dreams as creating the lightest chair hold no interest for him, he nonetheless relishes coming up with such a design. Conversation between Wanders and the author, 16 May 2013.

11 A reference made by Wanders in an article by I. van der Linden. 'Hightech materialen, lowtech esthetiek', *Decorum*, 15 (1997) 4, 35-37, quote about the 'Egyptian model' on 36.

12 Ingeborg de Roode, 'Industriële Vormgeving / Industrial Design', *Aanwinsten / Acquisitions 1993-2003 Stedelijk Museum Amsterdam*, Amsterdam 2006, 98-105.

13 S. Calatroni, 'Destroy and Create', *Interni*, (1996) 463, 181.

Drawing of the *Knotted Chair* with a table and a lamp showing the textile aspect, c. 1996, felt pen on paper, collection of the designer

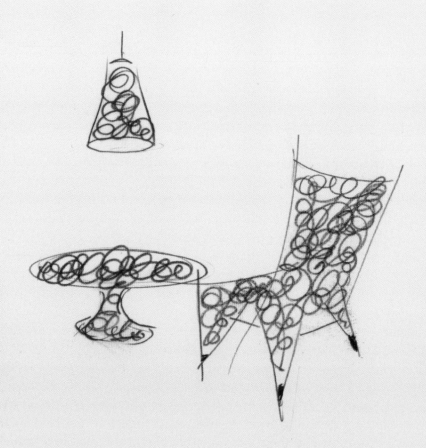

14 L. Young, 'Making a Statement with "Mutant Materials"', *New York Times*, 24 April 1996; *International Herald Tribune*, 27 April 1996; exh. cat. *Rotterdam Designprijs 1997*, Rotterdam 1997, cat. nr. 179; Tom Dixon, 'The ten best chairs', *The Independent*, 1 May 2002.

15 Both point out that it is hard to knot with the aramid cord, because it easily slops, but Wanders considers this to be an advantage, because it makes it possible to adjust the knots slightly during the process. Conversation between the author and Marleen Kaptein – now part of design studio Kapitein Roodnat, at the time an intern for Wanders, 30 August, 2013, and conversation with Wanders, 2 September 2013.

16 Wandschappen was founded in 1999 by Ivo van den Baar and Nicole Driessens in Rotterdam. Ivo van den Baar worked as a freelancer for Wanders on the *Knotted Chair* before he was put in charge of production in 1997 and he started working with Nicole Driessens. Conversation with Ivo van den Baar, May 2013.

Design Prize, the chair was referred to as a 'milestone'. In the *New York Times* and the *International Herald Tribune* it was described as 'groundbreaking', and fellow designer Tom Dixon included it a couple of years later in an exclusive list of 'the 10 best chairs'.[14] In 1996, Wanders was awarded the Kho Liang Ie incentive prize of the Amsterdam Fund for the Arts for the *Knotted Chair* and, in 1997, the public prize of the Rotterdam Design Prize. The model was also included in the Vitra Miniatures Collection, the hall of fame of furniture design.

At this point, Wanders had no employees, and produced the first models of the chair with an intern from the Design Academy.[15] When orders began flooding in in response to the huge success of the presentation in Milan – including those from numerous museums – an alternative was needed. At first, the chairs were made in Wanders' studio, with assistants hired from time to time. In 1997, production of the chair was taken over by the design and production studio Wandschappen, which is still responsible for its production.[16]

The *Knotted Chair* rapidly became one of the icons of the Droog collection, and of Dutch Design in general. Photographs of the chair were published so frequently that Wanders even remarked that the photograph had actually become more important than the object. Jongerius, too, concluded that her most well-known designs mostly seem to have a life in interior- and design magazines.[17] From around 1997, Wanders' studio and the Italian furniture manufacturer Cappellini,

The Knotted Chair   Ingeborg de Roode

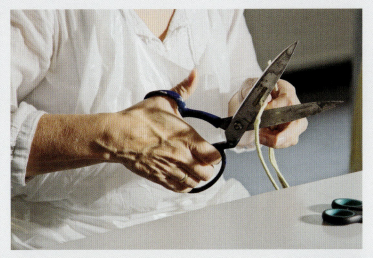
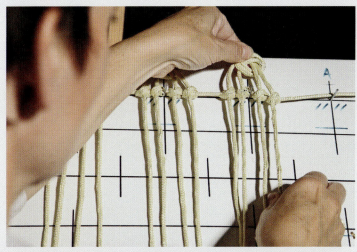

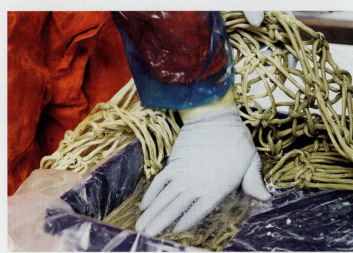

Different phases in making the *Knotted Chair* at Wandschappen in Rotterdam, 2013: cutting the cords, knotting, drenching in epoxy, finishing the legs while the knotted structure is hanged in a frame to be secured, the carbon is visible at the ends of the cords

Flying Knotted Chair, chair, 2006, Personal Editions, knotted aramide fibre cord with carbon core, secured with epoxy resin, sand blasted, pvc. Designed for the Abitare il Tempo Fair in Verona.

Knotted Chair, 1995-1996

Wanders made a number of gold, silver, white, black, and red versions of this successful design (the original chair was in the faded green shade of the aramid fibre) and a version suspended from a balloon, the *Flying Knotted Chair* (2006). He also designed a table in the same style, the *Knotted Table* (2001), and the *Fishnet Chair* (2001), which is hand-knotted but can also be industrially made. In fact, that chair comprises a tubular network that is indented to create a seat.

Knotted Table (prototype), table, 2001, Cappellini, knotted aramide fibre cord with carbon core, secured with epoxy resin (chromed), sand blasted, fibreglass top, coll. Textielmuseum, Tilburg

Fishnet Chair, chair, 2001, Personal Editions, knotted aramide fibre cord with carbon core, secured with epoxy resin, sand blasted

Knotted Chair (prototype no.5), lounge chair, design 1995-1996, knotted aramide fibre cord with carbon core, secured with epoxy resin, sand blasted, coll. Stedelijk Museum Amsterdam

which had taken the design into its collection that same year, began to use a photograph shot from a low angle in which the legs, now more streamlined than in the first series, stand on a horizontal line (see p. 119). Wanders believes that this angle shows the chair to its best advantage. Even then, he was extremely aware of the publicity value of good photography and strove for a canonisation of the image.

Despite its world-wide recognition, inclusion in numerous museum collections and all major survey publications on design, the *Knotted Chair* was not sold in amounts of tens of thousands. As the production of the 1000th chair approached, Wanders decided it was a nice round number, and it was time to take the chair out of production.[18] Those who are still interested in buying one need to be fast – although it may already be too late.

[17] Wanders in Robert Thiemann, 'Spinner of Tales', *Frame*, 17 (2000), 42, 44; Jongerius in J. Veldkamp, 'Dutch Design staat stil', *Elsevier*, Interior theme number, October 2003, 65-68, quote on 66.

[18] The *Knotted Chair* is available through Droog for € 3,630. The price and the fact that the chair is hardly used for its actual purpose probably explains why more copies of the design were not sold. Email from Marcel Wanders to the author regarding ceasing production, 10 September 2013.

Vista of apartment, restaurant and swimming pool, wine cellar and lobby (next pages) in apartment building Quasar, Istanbul, 2015

Quasar, 2015

The hall of this luxurious apartment building in Istanbul will contain a sculptural element with a European face on one side and an Asian face on the other (see also p. 48). It symbolises the position and culture of Istanbul as a bridge between two continents, Europe and Asia. The apartment walls are finished with a variety of three-dimensional treatments which enhance their tactility.

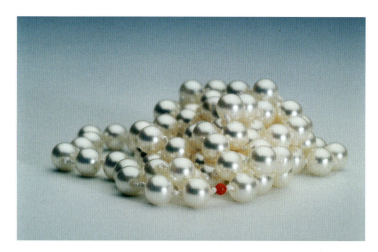

Marcel Wanders and Dinie Besems,
Pearl Necklace, necklace project, 1995,
pearls, string and several other materials

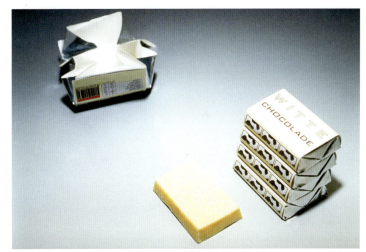

Pearl Necklace, 1995

Marcel Wanders met Dutch jewellery designer Dinie Besems at the exhibition 'De oogst' (The hearvest) at the Stedelijk Museum. They decided to collaborate on a series of jewellery and created eight *Pearl Necklaces*, each with its own story. According to Dinie Besems the aim was to position the pearl necklace in different contexts. For example a context of murder – in that case the necklace is the murderous weapon – , the context of another designer's work (the lable with the holes in it points to the Gatenproject (Holes Project) of Gijs Bakker) or music (Carolien Berkenbosch composed by special request of Wanders and Besems a piece of music). According to Wanders on the other hand, his aim was to 'demonstrate that form not always follows function and the truth in design is in fact a lie'(e-mail to the author 22 November 2013). After all, it turned out to be possible to give a new meaning to the necklace over and over again.

Marcel Wanders and Erwin Olaf, publicity from series *Double Portraits*, 2002, with *Crochet Table* (2001) of Marcel Wanders, Moooi, crochet cotton, secured with epoxy raisin, sand blasted

Crochet Table, 2001

This is the crocheted version of the *Lace Table* of 1997. The use of crocheted material rather than lace created a more robust construction. Wanders used the same material afterwards for a number of different designs: the *Crochet Chair* (2006), the *Crochet Light* (2007), and the *Crochet Courage* (2007). He also made black and chrome-coloured variants of the *Crochet Table*.

One Minute Sculpture, 2004

Wanders began making little sculptures in 2004. He says that while he and his daughter Joy were playing with clay, he happened to place a couple of similar shapes side by side. The sculptures were quick to make, had a fun spontaneity and, of course, were all slightly different. They were the perfect expression of Wanders' quest for a more individual, emotional, and 'humanist' design, the production of which can be repeated and controlled. Wanders set himself the task of creating a piece in one minute, had them glazed and gold-plated, and presented them as *One Minute Sculptures*.

One Minute Sculpture, object, 2004, Personal Editions, ceramics, glazed with gold luster

Living room and bedroom, Villa Amsterdam, private house, Amsterdam, 2008

Villa Amsterdam, 2008

This private house in Amsterdam is rife with textured surfaces from the two-tone parquet floor to the walls and ceilings.

Personal Editions exhibition, 2007

In 2007, Wanders launched the Personal Editions label with a big exhibition during the Milan Furniture Fair. The Personal Editions label includes pieces that are generally of a more experimental nature and are often produced in small editions. The pieces are made under the control of Wanders; with this practice he follows in the footsteps of the self producing Dutch designers.

Vice & Virtue, perfume and packaging, 2010, Cosme Decorte (Kosé), glass, metal

Vice & Virtue, 2010

In 1998, Wanders developed a perfume bottle for Cacharel with two separate parts. The design developed no further than the prototype. In 2010, Wanders returned to the concept. The fragrance he had developed for Cosme Decorte proved to be unstable; the ingredients needed to be separated. The perfume required a bottle with two individual compartments. This is the first dual-component scent; the actual fragrance is created when the two individual elements mingle on the skin.

Personal Editions presentation in Milan, 2007, with *Crochet Light* (2007), *One Minute Sculptures* (2004) and *One Minute Delft Blue Vase* (2006)

Making of *Topiary Mary* and *Bob* (below right) in the Wanders studio, 2007, Personal Editions. The crocheted parts are being pinned on the core, sewn together, then secured with epoxy and finished.

Topiaries, 2007

The art of topiary (sculpting shrubs into ornamental shapes) undergoes a remarkable, permanent transformation in these life-sized objects of crocheted cotton. The shapes need to be sculpted just once. The crocheted parts are carefully pinned to a polystyrene core, stitched together, soaked in epoxy and secured. After hardening, the core is removed. This is how *Bob*, *Frank*, *Mary*, and *Sid* were created – fascinating transparent anthropomorphic objects frozen in time.

Topiary Mary, 2007, Personal Editions, handmade cotton crochet, secured with epoxy resin, sand blasted

Westerhuis, office space, with *Moosehead* (2008) in big meeting room (top) and hallway with the *Dandelion*-hanging lamp (2004) by Richard Hutten for Moooi, Amsterdam, 2008

Westerhuis, 2008

The former school in the Jordaan quarter of Amsterdam was founded as a platform for the creative industries by Wanders and project developer Paul Geertman of Aedes Real Estate. Wanders' studio, where a team of 50 works, occupies the top two floors of the five-storey building. Moooi has its showroom on the ground floor. The other floors are home to all kinds of creative companies and studios. Since completing the Lute Suites project in 2005, Wanders has been regularly involved in real estate development. He was co-owner of Lute, and is now part owner of the Andaz Hotel.

Publicity photo for *Cyborg Wicker*, chair, 2010, Magis. Art direction: Marcel Wanders

Cyborg, 2010

Echoing science fiction cyborgs – beings that blend the human with the machine – this furniture combines industrially produced bases with handmade wickerwork seat backs – the perfect marriage of high and low tech. Also a variation with a plastic back is being produced.

Cyborg, chair, 2010, Magis, polycarbonate

Marcel Wanders' Most Important Designs — Ingeborg de Roode

Glass Bench, 2014, Personal Editions, sandblasted, tempered glass, cast iron

Glass Bench, 2014

This bench has the same pattern as the marble *Pizzo Carrara Bench*, which was presented in 2007 in Milan at the Personal Editions Exhibition. By sandblasting the pattern onto the inside of the thick glass, Wanders creates the impression of a crocheted volume floating inside the glass bench.

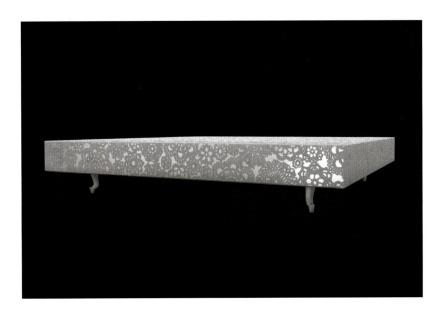

Pizzo Carrara Bench, 2007, Personal Editions

Egg Vases, 1997, Droog For Rosenthal / Moooi, partly glazed porcelain

Marcel Wanders and Erwin Olaf, *Eggeisha*, publicity photo from the series *Superheroes*, 2008

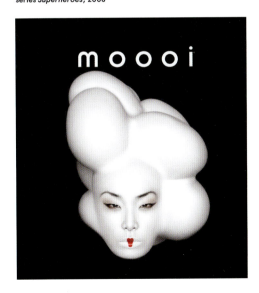

Egg Vase, 1997

During the project that Droog created for porcelain manufacturer Rosenthal, Wanders designed a number of classics such as this *Egg Vase*. He placed a handful of hardboiled eggs in a condom and made a mould based on three measurements. By glazing only the inside, the exterior of the vase has a delicacy reminiscent of an eggshell. Special versions were produced in 2003 (including gold- and silver-plated variants). In 2007, a version with the Interpolis pattern of bright flowers (2002) was made.

Mondrian South Beach Miami Hotel, hotel interior for Morgans Hotel Group (swimming pool with skyline of downtown Miami (top left), entrance area (bottom left), entrance hall with *Superhero* (top right), swimming pool with lounge area (far right), lobby with *Superhero* (right), Miami, 2008

Mondrian South Beach Hotel Miami, 2008

This is the first hotel Wanders designed for the renowned Morgans Hotel Group, famous for the hotel interiors of Andrée Putman and Philippe Starck. The girls (the *Superheroes*) who boldly gaze down at visitors, are a spectacular feature. Also particularly impressive is the outdoor space, which boasts a swimming pool encircled by spacious cabins where guests can relax and enjoy the skyline of Miami.

Villa Moda, multi-brand fashion store with *Zeppelin* (2005, far left), plaster dome (top), wooden flower shaped decoration on the wall (left) and walls of plastic balls (next pages), Manama (BH), 2009

Villa Moda, 2009

Wanders designed this vast store (1,050 square metres) with a shop-in-a-shop concept that features luxury brands to be an international souk. He explored local and international crafts, incorporating numerous craft elements into the final design. Wanders chose a restrained black-and-white palette to show off the jewel-hued Eastern clothing to best effect.

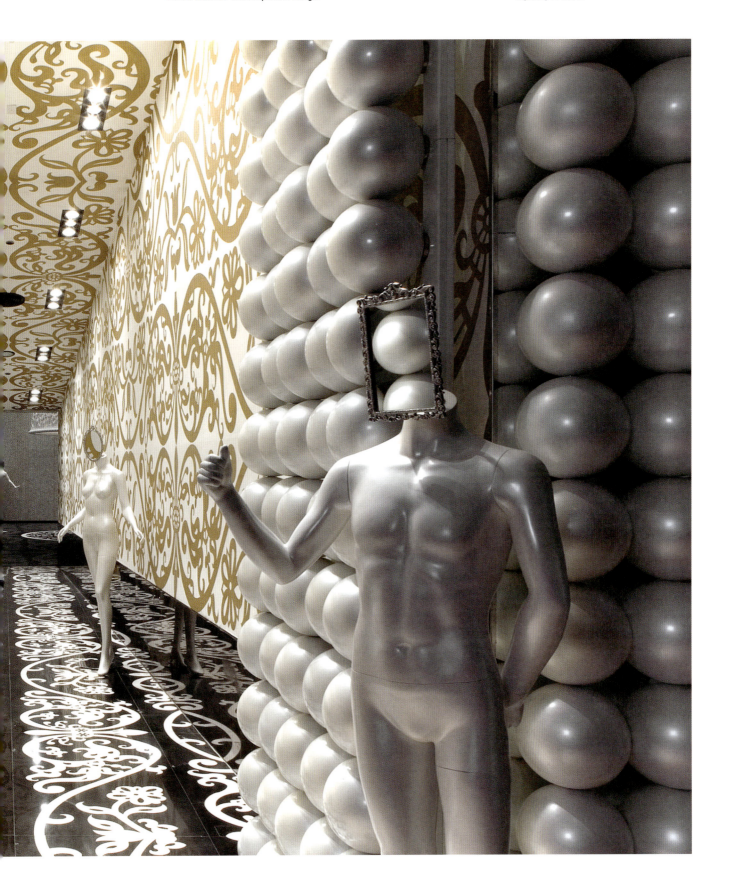

Make-up for Cosme Decorte, since 2010

Wanders has had his own cosmetics and skincare collection under the name *AQMW* with the Japanese brand Cosme Decorte since 2010. He not only designs the packaging, but also has a hand in selecting the items for the collections and deciding the contents, such as the colours of the lipsticks. Each year, the Japanese company Cosme Decorte launches special editions. For several years, Wanders has designed a powder compact for the company, in a limited edition. In 2013, the compact took the form of a box with a porcelain bell as a lid, and a series of bells that fit inside one another, like a clapper. The bell, a traditional symbol of communication and coming together, is one of Wanders' favourite themes. He uses the bell on different scales, large and small.

Marcel Wanders' Most Important Designs — Ingeborg de Roode

Collection make up and packaging for skin care products for *AQMW*, 2010, Cosme Decorte (Kosé), various materials

Bell Deco, limited edition face powder, packaging, 2013, Cosme Decorte (Kosé), painted and glazed ceramic, gold-plated metal

Limited edition face powder, packaging, 2011, Cosme Decorte (Kosé), crystal, metal

153

Personal Editions-presentation in Milan, 2007, with among other things *Big Ben Bianco* (2007), *One Minute Delft Blue Sculpture The Farmer* (2006) and *Topiary Frank* (2007)

Giant Bells, 2007

In 2007, Wanders designed a series of objects such as a big bell with a bow. As autonomous objects they rest on the floor or they can hang as a lamp with a chandelier inside. In 2007, Wanders exhibited them for the first time during his Personal Editions exhibition in Milan.

VIP Chair, 2000

This chair was designed for the interior of the VIP space, the Royal Wing Room, of the Dutch pavilion which was designed by architecture and urban design firm MVRDV at the 2000 World's Fair in Hanover (see p. 174). The tailored upholstery – which looks a little like trouser legs – conceals tiny wheels, creating a fun detail for the user to discover.

Marcel Wanders and Erwin Olaf, publicity photo from the series *Double Portraits*, with the *VIP Chair* (2000), Moooi, 2002

Publicity photo for *European* and *World Business Class Tableware*, in-flight service for KLM, 2010. Art direction: Marcel Wanders

World Business Class Tableware, inflight service for KLM, 2011

Old and new (left) waterglass for KLM, 2011, respectively 2013, glass, borosilicate glass. The new glass is 30% lighter

European and World Business Class Tableware, 2011

After more than 20 years, a set of Wanders' in-flight tableware was finally produced for Dutch airline KLM. Wanders was first asked to come up with a design for KLM in 1989. Design bureau Landmark was awarded the project at the time. They offered Wanders a job, and asked him to refine their design. Although Wanders has worked on various prize-winning innovative in-flight tableware designs since then, including a set made of biodegradable plastic, his first entire set of tableware did not appear in KLM's business class until 2011.

B.L.O., 2001

How do you turn this little candlestick on and off? Simple – just blow. Wanders combined the archetypical shape with a streamlined look and innovative, user-friendly technology.

B.L.O., table lamp, 2001, Flos, polished stainless steel, translucent or opaque perspex

Rainbow Necklace, 2007

This kaleidoscopic necklace is made up of beads of various materials. Some are references to other designs by Wanders, or to materials he uses – the golden *Nosé* logo, a *One Minute*, blue delftware beads, mosaics from Bisazza and glass from Baccarat. One of the beads also holds a Viagra pill. Wanders himself often wears this necklace; he says that, with its references and stories, it's become a kind of personal journal.

1. Nosé
2. Murano
3. Red Sherazade
4. White Bead
5. One-Minute Bead
6. Fertility Bead
7. **HE** Bead
8. Little Blue & White
9. Little Blue & White
10. Knot
11. Folded Metal
12. Tiny Blue
13. Fertility Bead
14. Gummi
15. Gall Stone
16. Neissing
17. Viagra
18. Black Pearl
19. Fertility Bead
20. Black Nadja
21. White Flowery
22. Shooting Star
23. Red Glass
24. Black Beady
25. Baby Blue & White
26. Fertility Bead
27. Bisazza
28. Baccarat
29. Gold
30. Green Nadja
31. Fertility Bead
32. Lava Bead
33. Orange Bead
34. Time Bead
35. Green Dice

Rainbow Necklace, 2007, Personal Editions, various beads, Edition of 25

Calvin, floor lamp, 2007, Personal Editions, polyester, fabric

Calvin, 2007

This light was designed as a 'protective' night light to stand next to a baby's crib. However, the *Calvin* is so tall that it's impossible to reach the shade with the petticoat. The light and crib were first presented in the Poliform presentation 'My House of Dreams' (also designed by Wanders) in the Zona Tortona during the 2008 Milan Furniture Fair.

United Crystal Forest: (Rois de la forêt), vases, 2010, Baccarat, crystal, metal

United Crystal Forest, 2010

Deer-like metal creatures populate the *United Crystal Forest*. Other, more traditional, objects can be found there, too, including vases and a candelabra. Each of the designs combines handmade glass and metal.

(previous page) *United Crystal Forest: Spirits of The Forest*, tall deer, medium deer, small deer, floor candle holders, 2010, Baccarat, crystal, metal

The Carbon Balloon Chair Held up to the Light

Ingeborg de Roode

[1] For more on the drive to design lightweight furniture and how this ambition was influenced by the development of materials and techniques, see: I. de Roode, 'Form follows function? 150 years of furniture design', in: *Stedelijk Collection Reflections*, Rotterdam/Amsterdam 2012, 313-332.

[2] The furniture designs for which weights are provided are all in the collection of the Stedelijk Museum Amsterdam.

[3] Designs in the holdings of the Stedelijk Museum include the inflatable *Verkade Air Chair* (circa 1967) made from PVC that weighs only 1.2 kg; this is a variant of the famous *Blow* by De Pas, d'Urbino, Lomazzi & Scolari, also made from PVC, from the same year.

Michael Thonet, *No. 14*, 1859–1860/c. 1865, manufactured by Gebrüder Thonet, Vienna, bent and stained beech frame, woven split cane seat

With regard to the *Knotted Chair*, Marcel Wanders has always said he is not primarily interested in 'designer's dreams', such as making the lightest chair in the world. However, he does engage in the debate on this theme from time to time.

The interest – both literal and figurative – in 'light' furniture first peaked in the 1920s; Modernist designers strove to create furniture that would preserve the transparency of the space.[1] They pursued this ideal by designing tubular steel-framed furniture. By reflecting light, these designs appeared physically lighter than the dark bentwood furniture produced by manufacturers such as Thonet, which modernists had at first greatly admired. This optical lightness was of greater importance than the actual weight, because numerous chair designs produced in wood actually weigh much less than their modernist metal counterparts: Thonet's model *No. 14* (1859-1860) weighs around 2.6 kg, and a traditional Italian-made *Chiavari* chair (circa 1845) is only 1.6 kg, while even the simplest tubular steel designs by Marcel Breuer (such as the *B33* of 1927-1928) and Mart Stam weigh 4 kg.[2] Aluminium furniture, which came onto the market in the late 1930s (for example the *Landi* chair by Hans Coray, 1938-1939: 3.0 kg), afforded greater 'lightness' but, by the late 1950s, one of the lightest chair designs was still manufactured in wood: the elegant *Superleggera* (1951-1957) by Gio Ponti. The chair, the title of which clearly expresses Ponti's intention (in English, 'Super Light'), weighs in at just 1.7 kg.

With the exception of experiments with card and paper (such as those of Frank Gehry), the introduction of new materials proved particularly effective in minimising weight. The inflatable plastic furniture that emerged at the end of the 1960s was light by its very nature; some armchairs weigh a little over 1 kg, thus making them the next high point in the quest for lightness.[3] Over the last two decades, it has become clear that carbon fibres and composites offer enormous potential, thanks to their strength at a relatively low weight. Leaving inflatable furniture out of the picture, Wanders' *Knotted Chair*, in which he utilises a

Carbon Balloon Chair, chair, 2013, Personal Editions, woven carbon fibre, blown, secured with epoxy resin, sand blasted

Making of the prototypes of the *Carbon Balloon Chair* in the Marcel Wanders Studio (inflating woven carbon balloons, custom cutting carbon balloons, coating with epoxy, bending of the balloons), 2013

4 I. de Roode, 'Bertjan Pot', *Stedelijk Museum Bulletin* (2005) 1, 30-32.

composite of carbon and aramid, is one of the lightest lounge chairs I know (see pp. 118–125); it weighs only 1.4 kg.

Ordinary chairs are generally less heavy than lounge chairs. The *Carbon Copy* (2003), a design by Bertjan Pot, which is the inspiration for the *Carbon Chair*, on which Pot and Wanders collaborated for Moooi (see p. 26), weighs a little less than the *Knotted Chair*, namely 1.2 kg. Like many other designers before him, Pot is fascinated by the possibilities of transparency and weight minimisation that carbon offers him.[4] The weight of the *Carbon Copy* approaches the almost-magical limit of 1 kilo. That limit was first achieved in 1987, when Alberto Meda designed the *Light Light* chair. This chair, which was produced in a limited edition by manufacturer Alias, consists of a Nomex honeycomb core between two layers of carbon – an early example of a composite with a sandwich construction. Marcel Wanders' *Carbon Balloon Chair* of 2013 is one of the few designs to convincingly defy the weight limit: the chair weighs approximately 800 grams.

Wanders uses balloons of woven carbon, which are filled with compressed air then hardened with epoxy, from which they derive their sturdiness. Wanders also used compressed air to fill volumes and create a light, yet robust, construction in the *Sparkling Chair* of 2010 (see p. 80). The design can be compared to PET bottles in which the bottle owes its firmness to the carbonated drink – but only as long as the lid is closed. In the *Carbon Balloon Chair*, the sturdy structure is achieved by using epoxy. The ends of the balloon that form the ring of the chair seat are attached to each other at the back; the ends of the balloons forming the legs and chair back are secured in the ring of the seat, which was hardened beforehand. The transparent seat is created from a grid of carbon.

Making of the prototypes of the *Carbon Balloon Chair* in the Marcel Wanders studio (attaching a leg to the ring of the seat, nailing the seat), 2013

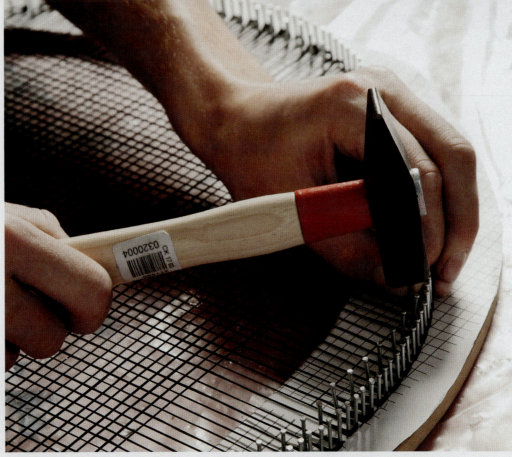

Making of the prototypes of the *Carbon Balloon Chair* in the Marcel Wanders studio (finishing), 2013

The balloon shapes bring to mind the balloon dogs that clowns make, as well as the *Balloon Dogs* of Jeff Koons. Wanders, however, colours the chair matt black, while the clowns, and Koons, always use bright hues.

The *Carbon Balloon Chair* is made by hand, and is thus only available in a small edition. In addition to the chair, Wanders is also working on designs for a bar stool and a cabinet. Although it was probably not his original intention, after his *Knotted Chair*, Wanders is another step closer to creating the world's lightest chair – an ideal that originated almost a century ago. On an industrial scale, the production of ever-lighter furniture has certain benefits – if it requires fewer materials and, consequently, generates less waste, can be rapidly produced, and/or transported more cheaply. It also has advantages in terms of project furniture, which needs to be frequently repositioned and removed. For standard domestic use, whether a chair weighs one kilo or three is of little importance. Super-light furniture may present its own dangers – a chair could easily tip over when someone is about to sit down. Designers face the challenge of making improvements that are also applicable within a more general context. We will need to wait and see if Wanders' discovery of inflating, and hardening, carbon balloons will eventually lead to a more general application of this kind. For the time being, it remains a remarkably intriguing experiment that has given birth to an astonishing design.

Corona de Agua, crown (prototype), 2001, polished silver, designed for the competition of the Museum Het Kruithuis

Corona de Agua, 2001

In 2001, to celebrate the engagement of Máxima and Prince Willem-Alexander, Museum Het Kruithuis in 's-Hertogenbosch organized a competition to design a tiara for Máxima. The contest attracted many distinguished designers. The prize was awarded to Ted Noten, who created a helmet for Prince Willem-Alexander with a detachable tiara for Máxima. Marcel Wanders created an extraordinary crystal tiara, freezing time poetically, in a way that celebrated Máxima's significance to the Dutch nation, and the role of her future husband.

Moosehead, sculpture, 2008,
Personal Editions, glazed ceramics

Moosehead, 2008

Following the *One Minutes* principle, working to a strict time limit, Wanders also made the ceramic *Mooseheads* to be wall-mounted. The *One Minutes* concept he also used for *Delft Blue* (see p. 96), the *One Minute Plates*, and in 2010 he made the *One Minutes Baccarat*, in which he combined ceramics with glass.

Publicity photo for *Dressed Pots & Pans*, 2012, Alessi. Art direction: Marcel Wanders

Dressed, 2011

This extensive collection is typified by the attention lavished on the skin of objects. The surfaces are decorated in relief. The cutlery and a number of plates are decorated on the underside, for a surprising tactile experience. The greater an object's 'ceremonial' function, the richer the decoration.

Publicity photo for *Dressed*, collection of tableware and glass service, 2011, Alessi. Art direction: Marcel Wanders

Lunch lounge for furniture store Co van der Horst, Amstelveen, 1999, on picture above amongst others things Wanders' own *Big Shadows* (1998) and the *Knotted Chair* (design 1995-1996) and on picture below the toilets

Lunch Lounge, 1999

This is considered Wanders' first interior design. The Co van der Horst furniture store commissioned Wanders to design a lounge combining his own work and that of others. The most extraordinary feature was the bathroom: he placed three toilets side by side in an open space.

Lunch Lounge, restaurant/showroom for Co van der Horst, Amstelveen, 1999 with *Thinking Man's Chair* (1986) by Jasper Morrison in the foreground and Wanders' *Nomad Carpet* (1998) in the background, both for Cappellini

Babel, chair, 2010, XO, polycarbonate, turned wood

Babel, 2010

The *Babel* chair is made of just six parts, and it can be packed and transported in a flat box, which makes it perfect for Internet sales. It is a modern version of the super-functional and super-transportable chair *No. 14* by Thonet of 1859 (see p. 162). The French company XO was preparing to expand the *Babel* collection before it went bankrupt. Consequently, no further designs were added. With its legs in the form of traditional turned wood, the design fits into the *New Antiques* family.

Royal Wing Room, **Dutch Pavilion, Expo 2000, Hanover, Germany, 2000, with** *VIP Chair* **(2000) and** *Lucy* **candlestick (1999)**

Royal Wing Room, 2000

During the 2000 World's Fair in Hannover, a VIP room was placed on top of the Dutch pavilion with stacked landscapes by architecture and urban design firm MVRDV. Wanders was invited to design the space. He designed a 'sky' studded with metal detailing for the arched ceiling. On the polished floor, which was shaped like an ice rink, his *VIP Chairs* were arranged around a table that was draped in a glittering silver tablecloth, which he had designed in collaboration with the Netherlands Textile Museum in Tilburg.

Jardin d'Eden, 2010

Wanders began his working relationship with Christofle by designing cutlery and under plates, the core business of the company. In the art direction for the publicity photos he connects the decoration on the objects to tattoos. He has since designed larger objects, too, such as occasional tables made from metal.

Publicity photos for *Jardin d'Eden*, collection underplates and cutlery, 2010, Christofle. Art direction: Marcel Wanders

The Hotel On Rivington / Thor, bar (left), design with secret room (left) and entrance to restaurant (top). Styling: Tatjana Quax, New York, 2007

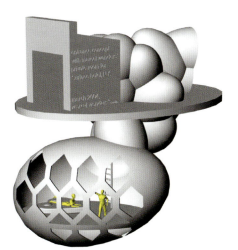

Thor, 2007

Wanders designed the bar and restaurant of this hotel on the Lower East Side of New York. His *New Antiques* furniture series was created during this project. The hexagonal wallpaper elements, which can be used in various positions to create playful and varied effects, were also specially designed for this project. Wanders had planned a secret space beneath the passage connecting the bar and restaurant; however, it still remains a mystery as to whether this was actually built or not.

Marcel Wanders applying an *Impressions* floor at the Westerhuis

Impressions, flooring, 2010
Senso, biopolymers, with *Smoke Chair* (2002) by Maarten Baas

Impressions, 2010

Wanders makes no attempt to hide his admiration of trompe l'oeil paintings. The surface of this Senso floor appears to be almost three dimensional, but the raised impression is created by its transparent coating. The flooring's surface is actually completely smooth.

Bella Bettina, 2010

In 2007 Wanders designed a serie of *Giant Bells*, all with a title including 'Bella' and a woman's name. Except for one, which stayed all white, the bells were painted by hand. *Bella Bettina* shows a pattern that refers to similar flower patterns which Wanders has often used since 2002.

Personal Editions presentation in Milan, 2007, with amongst others *One Minute Delft Blue Vases* (2006) and *Bella Bettina* (2007)

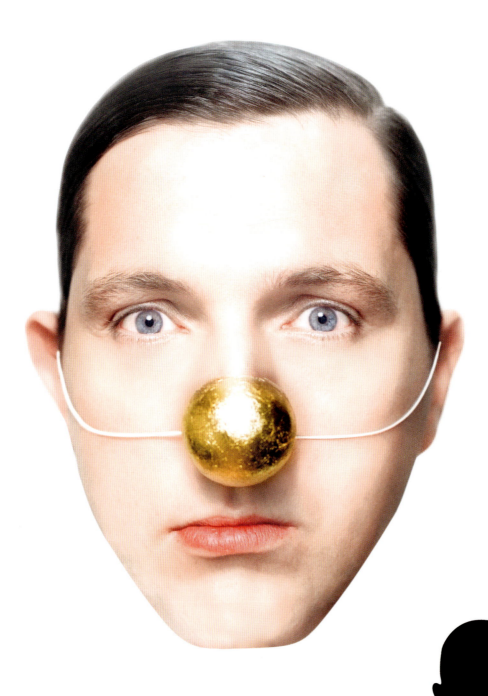

Nosé, 2002

In 2002, the *Nosé*, a golden clown's nose that can also be worn as a necklace, was created for the Dutch jewellery design company Chi ha Paura...?. After Wanders wore it in a portrait published on the cover of the French magazine *Intramuros* (see p. 59), the design began to lead a life of its own. The powerful image of Wanders wearing the nose appeared in numerous guises: a black logo in negative, incorporated into the *Jester* fabric (2006), a keychain, an art print, and a new version of the portrait almost a decade later.

Logo of Marcel Wanders with *Nosé* in negative, 2006

Portraits with *Nosé*, 2002 (left) and 2011 (right).
Art direction: Marcel Wanders

Logo of *Nosé*, 2010

Phoebe, 2013

The *Phoebe* light objects of 2013 consist of textile structures that integrate light. The objects are worn as a collar by a naked woman or, when not in use, presented on a stand. However, the nucleus of these works is the video, in which the object is shown in use.

Phoebe 2, floor lamp, 2013
Personal Editions, polyether foam painted in an acrylic paint, spinnaker cloth, polyamide, cotton, steel, leds

Phoebe 4, floor lamp, 2013
Personal Editions, mohair weave,
monofil, led lights, steel wire

Marcel Wanders Has a Dream

Pietje Tegenbosch

Marcel Wanders has a dream. It is a dream he has pursued as a product designer as well as an art director, an interior designer, a project developer, and, now, as an artist. At his exhibition at the Stedelijk Museum, Wanders is presenting his artwork for the first time. For several years, he has experimented with spatial objects in the context of specific interior projects such as Casa Son Vida on Mallorca (2008) and the Quasar building in Istanbul (scheduled for completion in 2015, see p. 127). Working on projects of this kind it was clear that, like some other designers and fashion photographers, Wanders sees the progression to the visual arts as a natural, almost organic, extension of his activities. Now he is presenting a series of video works entitled *Virtual Interiors*; these are muted images of constructed spaces.

  Wanders' email signature is short and snappy: Marcel Wanders - designer of a new age. The word 'designer' needs to be interpreted in the broadest sense of the word: Wanders designs, he creates a world, a construction with a story. His longing to share something, to tell something, resounds in the echo of his creativity. Storytelling is as old as humankind; it is a tool that can give substance and shape to our lives. Classical stories – whether they are those of the Bible, the *Odyssey*, or *One Thousand and One Nights* – have defined how we think. Each one of these stories has been retold again and again, down the years, charged with new meanings. Stories are not meant to 'entertain'; first and foremost, they are intended to create order in the chaos we call life that confronts us with big questions and implies both joy and sorrow.

  Wanders has a dream. His stories do not concern objects; instead, they touch the mind and the heart. Wanders speaks of his activities as a designer in terms of looking for a loving and respectful relationship with the world. For him, design is a platform to express energy, joy and happiness. This emphasis on the positive increasingly demanded a counterpoint, another colour, another work, another language, a new platform – a new age.

Wanders' new age is an era of unexpected possibilities, an era of a new artistic imagination. In his visual artwork Wanders searches for attention for the other side, the darker side, the side of doubt, sadness, fear – the blackness of the ultimate threat of finality.

If all goes well, an encounter with art sparks a surprising, unanticipated free fall through empty space. And the effect of that fall may come close to what Alice experienced when she tumbled into Wonderland. Perspectives are distorted; everything topples and shifts. Past, present and future blend in a vision of possibilities. Gradually Wanders came to the realisation that there were forces present in his work that, up to then, he had not made visible. Experiments with the moving image created new avenues for exploring notions of temporality and sustainability. For the first time, through the medium of the immaterial, Wanders was able to grasp his striving for sustainability and achieve a form of immortality through his work.

As 1926 drew to a close, Walter Benjamin wrote the following observation in his *Moscow Diary:* 'One only knows a spot once one has experienced it in as many dimensions as possible. You have to have approached a place from all four cardinal points if you want to take it in and, what's more, you also have to have left it from all these points. Otherwise it will quite unexpectedly cross your path three or four times before you are prepared to discover it. [...] The same with houses.'

The same is also true for an exhibition such as this in the Stedelijk Museum, and for the *Virtual Interiors* as well: you need to approach these works from different vantage points if you are to discover Wanders' dream.

186-187: *Virtual Interiors, German room, Wieliczka Salt Mine, Poland,* digital video, 2011-2013
188-189: *Virtual Interiors, Last Gypsfulvus' Room, Srinagar, India,* digital video, 2011-2013
190-191: *Virtual Interiors, Tilikums' Pool Tauranga, New Zealand,* digital video, 2011-2013

Death Is My Friend, art print, 2008,
Personal Editions / Luminaire, print

Death Is My Friend, 2008

Here, Wanders gently makes fun of himself by turning his logo (the abstract head with clown nose, in negative) into a death's head with its golden clown nose framed by intertwining tendrils. The rather macabre skull hints at Wanders' dark side, which has only emerged in recent years. It adds a new depth to the designer's ever-present optimism.

Oeuvre 1985 - 2013

Ingeborg de Roode in collaboration with Roos Hollander (Marcel Wanders Studio)

The lists on the following pages present an overview of the complete oeuvre of Marcel Wanders from 1985 to the present. The work is grouped into four categories: product and jewellery design, interior design, art direction and other projects.

The information is provided in the following order:
Title, description, year of first production or completion of design (in the case of designs that did not go into production), manufacturer (produced by / means a series of successive manufacturers), materials and techniques that may have influenced the design's appearance, 'NP' stands for 'no longer in production' and 'P' for 'still in production', client (if different from the manufacturer) or other information.

Product and Jewellery Design

Projects relating to product and jewellery design. This list contains all products in the field of jewellery design (both unique pieces and prototypes, as well as objects industrially produced in small series), all of which at least reached the stage of definitive design, or are known through publication. The list starts from Wanders' days as a student.

Mobilis, lounge chair, 1985
Artifort, pressed wood and metal, lacquered, rubber, upholstery, NP

Wearable Objects, three pieces of jewellery (unique pieces), 1985-1986
aluminium, plastic
Designed on the occasion of 10 years Vereniging van Edelsmeden en Sieraadontwerpers (VES)

Dipstick, dissolving coffee stick (model), 1986
Nescafé, instant coffee, plastic

Olea Europaea, Olympic awards (prototypes), 1986
wood, metal, gold leaf
Commissioned by Olympic Design 8692 Competition

Own Prize, ceramic object (unique piece), 1986
Olympic Design Competition, ceramic
Made after Olympic Design 8692 Competition

Chair for W.A. van Buren, model of a chair, 1986
various materials

Lijstbroche, brooch, 1987
(painted) metal, gold leaf, plastic, NP
Commissioned by Galerie Ra

Rijksappel, object (unique piece), 1987
various materials, NP

design for juice can / vase, 1987
glazed ceramic

ceramic shot cups, 1987
ceramic, 2k filler, copper, rubber, concrete

Dancing Is Fun For Two / Salt É Peppa, salt and pepper shakers, 1987
Marcel Wanders / Buys / DMD, ceramic, metal, NP

Ephese, pitcher / vase, 1987
Tichelaar, glazed ceramic, NP

Pillow Platters, series of ceramic products, 1987
Tichelaar, glazed ceramic, NP

Bad Black Box, box, 1987-1988
brass, rubber

Console, console (unique piece), 1987-1988
concrete with lava granules, lacquered wood

lounge chairs (unique pieces), 1987-1988
metal, Kvadrat woollen fabric, leather

lamp with concrete foot (prototypes), 1987-1988
aluminium, lycra microfibre, metal, plastic, white concrete with lava granules

file folder with clips, 1988
Albracht Systemen, pvc-covered cardboard, plastic, NP

collection of snacks (models), 1988
potato
Designed at the studio of BRS Premsela Vonk during an internship with Gijs Bakker

Millstone Lamp, table lamp, 1988
satin, chromed metal, cast iron, NP

Archie Bunker, desk lamp, 1988
rubber, lycra, tin-plated metal, rvs, NP
Commissioned by PTT (Dutch Post)

Theoliet, desk lamp, 1988
glass, copper, terracotta, eternit, NP
Commissioned by PTT (Dutch Post)

lamps, 1989
Buys Neon, various materials, NP

design for in-flight service for KLM (prototypes), 1989
De Ster, various materials

Wapper, umbrella, 1989
aluminium, treated polyester, NP
Commissioned by Galerie Coumans

Set Up Shades, floor lamp, 1989
Indoor / Droog / Moooi, cotton on a metal frame, later plastic, pvc/viscose laminate on metal frame, P in three sizes

Award for Stichting Industrieel Ontwerpen Nederland (iON), 1989
ashlar stone, NP
Commissioned by Stichting iON

Bethlehem, hanging lamp, 1989
laboratory glass, plastic

Pot's (Products of Timeless Scope), decorative objects (unique pieces), 1989
mdf, brass

signage, 1990
linoleum, wood, plastic
Commissioned by Apple for Europe Apple 1 Conference

Projectstoel Wim, **chair, 1990**
Car Industrie Katwijk, tubular steel, wood, NP

Amulet, **jewellery, 1990**
various materials
Commissioned by Galerie Marzee

Comb **(unique piece), 1990**
mdf, photoprint, copper, rvs, mirror, NP
Commissioned by Galerie Marzee

Marcel Wanders for Landmark, pregnancy test, 1990
Organon Teknika, polystyrene, NP

100 Castles in the Air, **wall object, 1990**
Marcel Wanders / Via Foundation, ceramic, etched magnesium, beech, copper, satin, NP

Couple, **vase, 1990**
Tichelaar, glazed ceramic, sand-lime brick, beech, copper, NP

Hero Pin, **pin, 1991**
lacquered magnesium, NP
Commissioned by Galerie Ra

Schaapjeslampje, **bedroom lamp, 1991**
Lumiance, messing, zinc plated steel, beech, screen printed (glow in the dark ink), metal, NP

Jubileummunt 1991, **coin, 1991**
metal, NP
Commissioned by Ministry of Finance

Vroomlamp, **floor lamp (unique piece), 1991**
artificial flowers, metal, pressed water resistant wood, cast iron

Armory Fish **and** *Armory Eggs* **(unique pieces), objects, 1991**
wood, various materials

Tears Tank (For Men Only) **and** *Time Eating Machine*, **tables (unique pieces), 1992**
painted wood, galvanised metal, Commissioned by Galerie Marzee

Trix, Lollypop, Wax, **floorlamps, 1992**
Heneka & Goldschmidt, nickel plated steel, textile (different types), P *Trix* at Moooi

clock, 1992
Pekago, injection-moulded ABS, NP

Glasbak, **glass bottle, 1992**
glass, cork, NP

Haikus, **objects (unique pieces), 1992**
various materials on wood

Naambroche + Box, **brooch and box (unique pieces), 1992**
paper, plastic, metal, wood, NP

Françoise van den Bosch Award, **1992**
wood, metal, cardboard, pearls, textile, NP
Commissioned by Stichting Françoise van den Bosch

Marcel Wanders for Landmark, *Wing*, **split airconditioner, 1992**
Stork, various materials, NP

Marcel Wanders for WAAC's, *Tulips* **(models), snacks, 1992**
rice, herbs

Tables and lighting for B. Ouwerkerk, 1993
Commissioned by B. Ouwerkerk, various materials

Identical Pins, **framed images, pin (unique piece), 1993**
various materials

Dutch Foil, **bookmarker, 1993**
silver-plated metal, NP
Commissioned by PTT (Dutch Post)

Diary clip, 1993
silver plated metal, NP
Commissioned by PTT (Dutch Post)

Cufflinks, **1993**
messing, pebble, NP
Commissioned by Verwo Beton

Tangram, **game, 1993**
wood, concrete, cardboard, NP
Commissioned by Verwo Beton

Lange Jan, **game, 1993**
plastic, NP
Commissioned by Verwo Beton

Marcel Wanders voor WAAC's, diary clip, 1993
silver plated metal, NP

medal, 1994
brass, NP
Commissioned by Anjerfonds

Fine Wearers, **brooches, 1994**
silk screen printed magnesium, NP
Collaboration with Indra Wildmann

Salt É Peppa, **salt and pepper shakers, 1994**
DMD, glass, NP

Saucers To Hang Up, **coat rack, 1994**
DMD, ceramic, plywood, NP

Pots, **table, 1994**
Montis, ceramic, glass, NP

Cutting Board, **cutting board, 1994**
wood, NP

Card Case, **card holder, 1994**
Marcel Wanders / Moooi, ABS, polypropylene, NP
Commissioned by Stichting Kunst en Bedrijf

vase, 1994
glazed ceramic, NP
Commissioned by Ministry of VROM

Gilde / Andries, **candlestick, 1995**
Cappellini, silver plated glass, NP

Pearl Necklace **(unique pieces), necklace project, 1995**
pearls, string and several other materials, NP
Collaboration with Dinie Besems

in-flight service for KLM City Hopper, 1995
Disc & Partners, bio-degradable plastic, NP

Hollow Casks, **vases, 1995**
DMD, ceramic, NP

Little Island, **pen tray and picture frame, 1995**
Pekago, injection-moulded ABS, rvs, NP

***Haasvaas*, vase, 1995**
Wanders Wonders, metal, NP

***De Voogt Clip*, clip, 1995**
De Voogt Systemen, polypropylene, NP

***Le Classeur*, folder, 1995**
De Voogt Systemen, recyclable plastic, P

***Knotted Chair*, lounge chair, 1996**
Droog, Cappellini, Personal Editions, carbon and aramide fibre cord, secured with epoxy resin, sand blasted, P
Edition of 1000 copies

***Mon Cheri*, cupboard (unique piece), 1996**
Wanders Wonders, glass, cardboard boxes
Commissioned by Galerie Ra

***Wedding Rings + Honeymoon Rings* (unique pieces), rings, 1996**
Wanders Wonders, gold, lacquered gold
Commissioned by Galerie Marzee

***1 Liter Vaas*, vase, 1996**
Wanders Wonders, silver-plated glass, NP

***B-Beker*, cup, 1996**
Wanders Wonders, glazed ceramic, NP

***Breakfast of a Dwarf Rabbit*, necklace, 1996**
Wanders Wonders, gilded silver, polyamide, NP

***Tape Necklace*, necklace, 1996**
Wanders Wonders, tape with box of cardboard, NP

***Pure Nature I*, six porcelain vases, 1996**
Rosenthal / Thomas, porcelain, NP

***Amsterdam Capital of Inspiration*, towel, object, 1997**
Wanders Wonders, cotton, printed sheet metal, NP
Commissioned by Amsterdams Fonds voor de Kunst

***Eurotop Gift*, bottle, cups, 1997**
Wanders Wonders, glass, stainless steel, NP
Commissioned by Amsterdams Fonds voor de Kunst

***Lace Table and Lace Table Black*, table, 1997**
Droog, Swiss lace (cotton), secured with epoxy resin, sandblasted, NP

***Egg Vase Small, Medium* and *Large*, vases, 1997**
Droog for Rosenthal / Moooi, partly glazed porcelain, P

***Ming Vase*, vase, 1997**
Droog for Rosenthal / Moooi, porcelain, P

***Foam Bowl*, bowl, 1997**
Droog for Rosenthal/ Moooi, porcelain, P

***Foam Bowl Special Edition*, vase, 1997**
Wanders Wonders, porcelain, NP

***Sponge Vase*, vase, 1997**
Droog for Rosenthal/ Moooi, porcelain, P

***Wanders Wonders Lighting Collection: Little Thin Light* (table lamp), *Folded Shade* (table lamp & hanging lamp), *Tall Thin* (table lamp), *Set Up Shades 2* (table lamp), *Setup Square* (table lamp), *Double Shade* (floor lamp), *Tree of Shadows* (floor lamp), *Big Wax* (floor lamp), 1997**
Wanders Wonders, pvc/viscose laminate on metal frame, some designs P

photo & address book, 1997
printed cardboard, metal, plastic, NP
Commissioned by Randstad

***Minature Knotted Chair*, model, 1997**
Miniatures Collection Vitra, carbon and aramide fibre cord, secured with epoxy resin, sand blasted, P

perfume bottle (prototype), 1998
metal, glass
Commissioned by Cacharel

Big Shadow floor lamps: *Little Big, Middle Big, Big, Extra Big*, 1998
Cappellini, metal, cotton or pvc, P

***Nomad Carpet*, carpet, 1998**
Cappellini, wool, wood, NP

***Trinity*, necklace, 1998**
Chi Ha Paura...?, silver, P

in-flight service, 1998
Disc & Partners, plastic, NP

***Medals*, 1998**
gold, silver, bronze, NP
Commissioned by Gay Games

***Tantra Pallet*, jewellery, 1998**
Wanders Wonders, plastic, paint, NP

***Wanders Wonders Lighting Collection* (additions), *Tube* (hanging lamp), *Setup Round* (table lamp), *Hang* (hanging lamp), *Tall Thin* (floor lamp), *Big Wide* (table lamp), 1998**
Wanders Wonders, pvc/cotton laminate on metal structure, some parts still at Moooi

***Schommeltrommel*, storage container, 1998**
Randstad, lacquered metal, NP
Commissioned by Randstad

***Bro's*, foam bowl, 1998**
Wanders Wonders, porcelain, NP
Commissioned by museum store Stedelijk Museum

hanging lamps, 1998
Wanders Wonders, aluminium, NP
Commissioned by Stichting Kunst en Cultuur Noord-Holland

***Willow Chair*, chair from the series *Couleur Locale for Oranienbaum* (prototype), 1999**
Droog, unpeeled willow shoot

***Apple Juice Bottle / Birdhouse*, apple juice bottle / birdhouse from the series *Couleur Locale for Oranienbaum* (prototypes), 1999**
Droog, ceramic

Birdhouse, birdhouse from the series *Couleur Locale for Oranienbaum*, 1999
Droog, wood (later: recycled polypropylene), porcelain, sisal, steel, P

Disposable Cutlery and Bowl, cutlery and bowl from the series *Couleur Locale for Oranienbaum* (prototypes), 1999
Droog, poplar wood, duplex pressed

Oranienbaumer Biscuits, biscuits from the series *Couleur Locale for Oranienbaum* (prototypes), 1999
Droog, cookies in cardboard

Oranienbaumer Viereck, bread from the series *Couleur Locale for Oranienbaum* (prototype), 1999
Droog, wholemeal orange loaf

Swing with the Plants, swing from the series *Couleur Locale for Oranienbaum*, 1999
Droog, wood, terracotta, rope, plant (later: polyethylene, polyamide rope), P

A Touch of Glass: Graniglia, bowl, 1999
Droog for Salviati, hand blown crystal, NP

Christmas Group, 1999
Wanders Wonders, cardboard cutouts, NP
Commissioned by *Eigen Huis Interieur*

Lucy, candlestick, 1999
Goods, injection moulded metal, P

Woonpin, pin, 1999
Wanders Wonders, metal, NP
Commissioned by HPR Techniek (Woonbeurs)

Dialogues, vases, 1999
Glass Factory Leerdam, glass, marble, stone, wood, NP

Liquid Experiments, glass objects (unique pieces), 1999
Glas Factory Leerdam, glass

Unity, vases, 1999
Glass Factory Leerdam, blown glass, NP

Wanders Wonders Lighting Collection (additions), ***Double Round Light*** (table lamp), ***Double Square Light*** (table lamp), ***Long Light*** (hanging lamp), ***Oval Light*** (hanging lamp), ***Round Light*** (hanging lamp), ***Square Light*** (hanging lamp), 1999
Wanders Wonders / Moooi, pvc/cotton laminate on metal structure, some parts still P

pencil sharpener, 1999
technical ceramic, NP
Commissioned by Museum Het Kruithuis

Jubilee Coin, coin, 1999
Wanders Wonders, metal, NP

SLS Vase, vase for the Municipality of Eindhoven (prototype), 1999
3D printed polyamide
For project Vaas voor de Gelegenheid (Vase for the Occasion)

Secretary Day Gift, cd and booklet, 1999
cardboard, chromolux, fotex, NP
Commissioned by Randstad

Halfvolle Glas-Actie, glass, 1999
cut glass, NP
Commissioned by Randstad

sanitary fittings and bathroom equipment (***Gobi***, bathtub and sink, shower ***Pipe***, sinks, taps and storage system), 2000
Boffi, Cristalplant, stainless steel, ceramic, anodized aluminium, P

Panpipes, hanging lamp, 2000
Cappellini, cotton and metal, NP

Setup Round, Setup Square, table lamps, 2000
Cappellini, cotton and metal, NP

Square Shadow, hanging lamp and table lamp, 2000
Cappellini, cotton and metal, P

Carpet sample catalogue, 2000
Desso, polypropylene, NP

Bottle Vitrine, vitrine, 2000
DMD, glass, metal, NP

Pebble, table / container, 2000
Magis, injection moulded ABS, P

Ultra Light Collection, lamps, 2000
Moooi, crepe georgette, metal frame, NP

VIP Chair, chair, 2000
Moooi, fire retardant foam covered steel frame, wool, polyamide, P

Symbolen van Klantvriendelijkheid, pins, 2000
metal with print, NP
Commissioned by the Municipality of Almere

Amsterdam Table, table, 2000
Wanders Wonders, etched stainless steel, NP

Big Shadow Special: Beast, Cow, Panther (unique pieces), floor lamps, 2000
Personal Editions, various materials

New York Table, table, 2000
Wanders Wonders, etched stainless steel, NP

January Gift / Olympic Games Sydney 2000 Gift, carafe, 2000
glass, plastic, NP
Commissioned by Randstad

Medical Care Day Gift, vase, 2000
glass, plastic, NP
Commissioned by Randstad

Thee voor in Bed Bad, tea bags, 2000
tea bags, NP
Commissioned by Randstad

Expo 2000, tablecloth and table runner, 2000
Netherlands Textile Museum, cotton, lurex, viscose, NP
The tablecloth was originally designed for the Dutch pavilion in Hanover; the runner as a derivation from this design especially for the Textile Museum

Relational gift from the Minister of Foreign Affairs, 2000
silver, crystal, porcelain, candles, NP
Commissioned by Netherlands Design Institute

Halo Lamp, hanging lamp, 2001
Cappellini, cotton, P

Knotted Chair Special: Future (Chromed), chair, 2001
Cappelini, knotted aramide fibre cord with carbon core, secured with epoxy resin, precious metal coated, NP

Knotted Table (prototype), table, 2001
Cappellini, aramide fibre, carbon, secured with epoxy resin (chromed)

Smoke, table, 2001
Cappellini, smoked glass, clear glass, P

Game, 2001
wood, NP
Commissioned by Eurowoningen

B.L.O., table lamp, 2001
Flos, polished stainless steel, translucent or opaque perspex, NP

Droog for Levi's, denim suits (male and female), 2001
Levi's, denim, NP

Murano Bags, shoulder bag, wallet, wristbag, knapsack, handbag, 2001
Mandarina Duck, sandwich of polyester foam, textile and metal NP

Crochet Table, table, 2001
Moooi, handmade cotton crochet, secured with epoxy resin, sand blasted, P

Double Decker, table, 2001
Moooi, American solid oak, stained and lacquered, P

Flower Chair, chair, 2001
Moooi, chromed aluminium, P

Flower Table, table, 2001
Moooi, luan wood with burnt-in flower illustration, NP

Mellow, chair, 2001
Moooi, European massive oak construction, hr foam upholstery stained and lacquered, NP

Omega Light, hanging lamp, 2001
Moooi, metal, NP

Phillipe (formerly known as *Gwapa*), chair, 2001
Moooi, galvanised and powder coated steel with polyethylene plastic webbing, stainless steel, NP

Splinter, vase, 2001
Moooi, crystal glass, blown and hand beaten, NP

Corona de Agua, crown (prototype), 2001
first prototype made in waterclear, second version in somos®9100, the last one in polished silver
For competition of Museum Het Kruithuis

Airborne Snotty Vase: Coryza, Influenza, Ozaena, Pollinosis, Sinusitis, vases, 2001
Personal Editions, 3D printed polyamide with the SLS technique, P

Airborne Snotty Vase Movie and Specials: Gold, Black and Painted (Interpolis Pattern), vases, 2001
Personal Editions, 3D printed polyamide with the SLS technique, Gold gilded, Painted painted, NP

Snotties / Blobs, objects, 2001
Personal Editions, gold lustered clay, glass, NP

Splinter Limited Edition: Black, vase, 2001
Personal Editions, crystal glass, blown and hand beaten, NP

Can of Gold: Hamburg (2001), *Washington* (2002), *Sydney* (2003), *London* (2003), *Mexico City* (2006), *Brugge* (2007), *Budapest* (2012), vases, 2001
Personal Editions, gilded sheet metal, P

Crochet Table Special, table, 2001
Personal Editions, handmade cotton crochet, secured with epoxy resin, sand blasted, NP

Fishnet Chair, chair, 2001
Personal Editions, hand knotted aramide fibre cord with carbon core, secured with epoxy resin, sand blasted, P

Fishnet Chair Special, chair, 2001
Personal Editions, carbon and aramide fibre cord, secured with epoxy resin, sand blasted, painted, NP

Knotted Chair Special: Black and White, lounge chair, 2001
Personal Editions, knotted aramide fibre cord with carbon core, secured with epoxy resin, sand blasted, NP

Stone Chair, lounge chair, 2001
Personal Editions / Cappellini, polyester, covered with silicone and pebbles, NP

January Gift, tea box, 2001
lacquered rubber wood, NP
Commissioned by Randstad

Medical Care Day Gift, glow in the dark cup, 2001
printed (with glow in the dark ink) polycarbonate, NP
Commissioned by Randstad

Smoke: Small, coffee table, 2002
Cappellini, glass, P

Wood, coffee table, 2002
Cappellini, chromed metal, press moulded maple, NP

Nosé, from Sense of Wonder collection, wearable object, 2002
Chi Ha Paura...?, gold-plated silver, P

Tableau Vivant for Prefet d'Alsace, dinner service and table decoration, 2002
Droog / Koninklijke Porceleyne Fles, various materials, NP

champagne glass, 2002
engraved glass, NP
Commissioned by Eurowoningen

award, 2002
moraine stone, gold/silver/
bronze plated, NP
Commissioned by Floriade

Bottoni, sofa, 2002
Moooi, multiple density foam,
plywood, stainless steel, P

**Bottoni Plaid: Orange Flower,
White Lace, Purple Flower,
Wild Fur, Blanket, Orange Woven,**
sofa covers, 2002
Moooi, various fabrics, NP

City, storage system, 2002
Moooi, powder coated steel, NP

Container, foot and table top,
2002 (with round top 2003)
Moooi, polyethylene, HPL, P

Mellow: Soft, chair, 2002
Moooi, plywood, hr foam
upholstered (or cmhr foam), NP

Oblique, mood board,
storage, 2002
Moooi, solid oak stained
and lacquered, P

January Gift, candy jar, 2002
glazed ceramic, wood, NP
Commissioned by Randstad

Gift for Temporary Workers,
chocolate and wine packagings
and suitcase, 2002
printed cardboard, NP
Commissioned by Randstad

December Gift, tray and glasses,
2002
Randstad, stainless steel,
anodized aluminium, NP
Commissioned by Randstad

Glass Design Competition,
Bombay Gin Martini glass
(prototype), 2003
glass
Commissioned by Bombay
Sapphire

Swarovski chandeliers
for Catshuis, 2003
crystal, NP
Commissioned by Ministry of the
Interior and Kingdom Relations

Host, wooden vases (design),
2003
Droog for TPM, wood

Patchwork, main course plates
(*Master, Gold Flower, Flag,
Pablo, Red Flowers, Gold Sun*);
underplates (*Dog, Sun, Little
Fish, Cherrie, Parsley, Little
Willie*); soup plates (*Gold Flower
Small, Child, Gold Flower Large,
Daily Bread, Tichelaar, Island*);
breakfast plates (*Dance, Circle,
Black Flower, Vortrag, Wrink,
Marcel Wanders*); side plates
(*Makkum, Chicken and Egg,
Foot, Eel, Coloured Lines,
Turtle*), 2003
Koninklijke Tichelaar Makkum,
painted and glazed ceramic, P

Eppo, chair (prototype), 2003
Magis, chromed steel,
polypropylene, textile

Flare, table, 2003
Magis, injection-moulded
polycarbonate, mdf with
polymeric top coat, P

Your Chair, chair, 2003
Magis, injection-moulded,
reinforced polypropylene,
metal wire, NP

*Bottoni Plaid: Grey Fur,
Grey Dot, Eclipse, White Flower,
Woven Flower*, sofa covers,
2003
Moooi, various fabrics, NP

Tracy, tray, 2003
Normann Copenhagen, stainless
steel, anodized aluminium, NP

Cuddles on the Run, toy car
(unique piece), 2003
Personal Editions, teddy bears,
secured with epoxy resin

Egg Vase Special, vase, 2003
Personal Editions, ceramic,
gilding, NP

Egg Vase Special, vase, 2003
Personal Editions, silver-plated
ceramic, P

Moooi Weer, golden bear
(unique piece), 2003
Personal Editions, porcelain bear,
gilding

*Sponge Vase Special:
Silver* and *XL*, vase, 2003
Personal Editions, glazed
(chromed) porcelain, NP

January Gift, photo frame, 2003
mdf, walnut, NP
Commissioned by Randstad

December Gift,
champagne glass, 2003
glass, NP
Commissioned by Randstad

Boblbee, back pack
(unique piece), 2004
plastics, textile, swiss lace, resin
Commissioned by Aids Fonds

Crystal, pen and cardholder,
2004
Acme, metal, printed pvc sheet,
NP

Designers Paint, paint, 2004
Alcro, water-borne eco paint, NP

T-Spoon, teaspoon for
Case da Abitare, 2004
Alessi, stainless steel, NP

Antelope, car (unique piece),
2004
Bisazza, glass mosaic

Coffee Table: Large and *Small*,
coffee table, 2004
Bisazza, glass mosaic, P

Bottoni Shelf, sofa, 2004
Moooi, mdf plywood, stainless
steel, P

Bottoni Slim, sofa, 2004
Moooi, mdf plywood, stainless
steel , P

Bertjan Pot in collaboration
with Marcel Wanders, *Carbon
Chair*, chair, 2004
Moooi, carbon fibre, secured
with epoxy resin, P

Container, stool, 2004
Moooi, polyethylene, P

Two Tops, secretary, 2004
Moooi, oak, mdf with oak veneer
top, P

Two Tops, table, 2004
Moooi, solid oak frame, mdf with oak veneer top, P

Woody, tea box, 2004
Normann Copenhagen, lacquered wood, NP

Celcius: Small, Table Model, Sport Model, water bottle (prototype), 2004
PET
Commissioned by private owner of a well

Hexagon, wallpaper, 2004
Personal Editions, fleece, silk screen, NP

One Minute Sculptures, sculpture, 2004
Personal Editions, clay, glazed with gold luster, P

The Lucky One, sculpture, 2004
Personal Editions, clay, glazed with gold luster, NP

Black and White Pattern, tiles, 2005
Art on Tiles, glazed ceramic, NP

Couples, pillows, 2005
B&B Italia, linen and printed cotton fabric, NP

Haikus, plates, 2005
B&B Italia, hand cast ceramic with hand applied polychrome print, NP

Still Life, centre piece, 2005
B&B Italia, glass, ceramic, NP

Ballerina, chair, 2005
Baleri, tubular steel, polyethurane, NP

The Wanders Collection. Bathtub and Sanitary Ware Soapbath Series, bathtub, wall hung bidet, wc, 2005 / 2011
Bisazza, fibreglass, P

The Wanders Collection. Accessories and Shower Taps Architectural Series, clothes hangers, towel rails, mirrors, furniture chandelier shower, 2005 / 2011
Bisazza, chrome-plated metal, resin, mirror glass, lacquered wood, crystal glass, P

Wallpaper, Snowflake Oro, Hermitage, wall tiles, 2005
Bisazza, glass ceramic tiles, P

Big Shadow Special: Extra Large Gold, floor lamp, 2005
Cappellini, metal, textile, gilded, NP

New Antiques, seating and tables, 2005
Cappellini, wood, foam, leather, crystal glass, P

Fioole, etagere, 2005
Cor Unum, stoneware, glazed, NP

Tassel, hanging lamp, 2005
Flos, metal, polyester, NP

Zeppelin, hanging lamp, 2005
Flos, cocoon of resin, crystal glass, perspex, steel, P

Kika Award, bear, 2005
porcelain, NP
Commissioned by Kika

Studio, desks, 2005
Lensvelt, melamine cheapboard, steel, epoxy, P

Little Flare, children's table, 2005
Magis, injection-moulded polycarbonate, mdf with polymeric cover, ABS, P

Boutique Blankets: January, May, September, November, bsofa covers, 2005
Moooi, polyester, cotton, polyamide, viscose, P

Boutique Covers: Chameleon Divina Melange 180, Chameleon Hallingdal 153, Coco, Daddy, Deer, Dior, Easy Rider, Kimono, Lace, Manga, Medaillon, New York, Silver, Sophy, Travis, Jester, Samurai, Snow White, sofa covers, 2005
Moooi, various textiles, P

Boutique Naked, sofa, 2005
Moooi, steel, cmhr foam, P

Frame, frame, 2005
Moooi, anodized aluminium, P

Frame Mirror, mirror, 2005
Moooi, extruded and anodized aluminium, mdf, mirror glass, P

Me?, mirror, 2005
Moooi, plaster with chrome finish, mirror glass, NP

Moooi Carpets: Square 1, 5, 11, carpets, 2005
Moooi, printed nylon threads, P

Naked Chair, chair, 2005
Moooi, oak stained and lacquered, NP

Naked Table, table, 2005
Moooi, oak, mdf, oak veneer, NP

Rectangle 3, 4, 6, 7, 10, carpets, 2005
Moooi, printed polyamide, P

July, throw, 2005
Moooi, printed cotton, NP

Flying Table, coffee table, 2005
Moroso, metal, wood, cotton, patinated bronze, NP

Print and **Print Pouffe**, sofa and pouffe, 2005
Moroso, wood, polyurethane and polyester fibre, P

Cristal, carafe and cups, 2005
Normann Copenhagen, glass, plastic, P

Rock, bowl, 2005
Normann Copenhagen, metal, NP

Tin Tin, container, 2005
Normann Copenhagen, lacquered metal, NP

Bears, 2005
Personal Editions, porcelain, NP

Spike-A-Delic Gala / Andy Warhol Museum, clogs (unique pieces), 2005
Personal Editions, painted wood

Dream, bed, 2005
Poliform, wood, upholstered, P

salad bowls, 2005
glazed ceramic, NP
Commissioned by Randstad

Gift for Temporary Workers, trolley, 2005
various materials, NP
Commissioned by Randstad

New Antiques, table, 2006
Cappellini, wood, aluminium, P

B.L.O. Special: Interpolis Pattern and *Black and White Flower Pattern*, table lamp, 2006
Flos, polished stainless steel, perspex, painted / cut out, NP

Sunflower Gold, flooring, 2006
Forbo, marmoleum, P

Gucci Bag, bag (unique piece), 2006
Gucci, leather, metal, fabric: polyester, polyamide, viscose

Happy Hour Chandelier, chandelier, 2006
Happy Hour Chandelier, various materials, P

Carrie, usb stick, *Crystal*, card reader, *Domino*, speaker system, *Egg*, speaker, *Mathilda*, wireless sound transmitter, *Merlin*, sound system transmitter, *Pandora*, media solution, frame flat tv, theatre & dvd, *Wave TV*, micro wave with built in dvd 2006
HE, various materials, NP

Stone, stool, 2006
Kartell, polycarbonate, P

Kika Painted Elephant, object, 2006
painted and glazed ceramic, NP
Commissioned by Kika

fruit bowl, 2006
carbon fibre secured with epoxy resin, NP
Commissioned by KPN

Container Bowl and *Container Bowl Top*, bowl and top, 2006
Moooi, polyethylene, P

Mannequin Dining: Black Jester, Feminine, Damask, chair, 2006
Moooi, powder coated steel, polyamide, silicon, polyester and cotton fabric, NP

Moooi Carpet Collection, carpet, 2006
Moooi, printed polyamide, NP

Wet Shadow, vase, 2006
Moooi, glass and stainless steel, NP

Zen, cupboard, 2006
Moooi, wenge, glazed ceramic, NP

3D Haikus: Fare un Bagno Nero, Un Occhiata Dietro il Nero, Uova Scure, Viaggio al di Fuori del Nero, objects, 2006
Personal Editions, polyamide, 3D printed with the SLS technique, NP

Flying Knotted Chair, chair, 2006
Personal Editions, knotted carbon and aramide fibre cord, secured with epoxy resin, sand blasted, pvc, NP

Big Shadow Special: Jester, floor lamp, 2006
Personal Editions, metal, polyester, polyamide, viscose, NP

Crochet Chair, chair, 2006
Personal Editions, crocheted rope, secured with epoxy resin, sand blasted, P

One Minute Plates, plates, 2006
Personal Editions, glazed and gilded ceramic, NP

One Minute Delft Blue, sculptures, vases, plates, 2006
Personal Editions, painted and glazed ceramic, P

Puppy Love, sculpture, 2006
Personal Editions / Luminaire, polyester, polyamide, viscose, NP
Designed to use together with *Puppy* by Eero Aarnio for Magis

Marcel Wanders by Puma Collection, The Villa (tent), *The Flip* (flip-flops), summer shopper, beach ball, bubble lounge, cool case, towel, 2006
Puma, various materials, NP

Beautiful Woman: Kate (cabinet), *Jen* (dressing table), *Paris* (mirror), *Ken* (side table and stool), 2006
Quodes, wood, veneer, brass, polyurethane, steel, glass, textile, P

Art Bag, bag, 2007
printed and woven polypropylene, NP
Commissioned by Stop Aids Now

Couples, pillows, 2007
B&B Italia, linen and printed cotton fabric, NP

Gold Collection, vase, stool, bowl, 2007
B&B Italia, ceramic, gold leaf, P

Haikus, plates, 2007
B&B Italia, hand cast ceramic with hand applied polychrome print, NP

Knotted Chair Special: Red, lounge chair, 2007
Cappellini, knotted carbon and aramide fibre cord, secured with epoxy resin, sand blasted, coated, NP
Edition of 99 on the occasion of 10 year anniversary of the design

World Carpets, carpet, 2007
Colorline, chromojet print on different textiles, P

Bertuno, sculpture, 2007
Cowparade, synthetic resin, P

Pin Up, wall stickers, 2007
Domestic, sticker, P

Skygarden, hanging lamp, 2007
Flos, aluminium, plaster, P

Sparkling, hanging lamp (prototype), 2007
Flos, glass

Matryoshka, stacking boxes, 2007
Habitat, plastified, printed cardboard, NP

Wallpaper, wallpaper, 2007
Habitat, printed paper, NP

tablecloth, 2007
viscose, damask, NP
Commissioned by Kika

Carved Chair, chair, 2007
Moooi, wood, hand carved, NP

Container, vase, 2007
Moooi, polyethylene, P

Mannequin Lounge: Black Jester, Feminine, Damask, chair, 2007
Moooi, powder coated steel, polyamide, silicon, polyester, cotton, NP

***Moooi Carpet: Square 2*, carpet, 2007**
Moooi, printed polyamide, NP

***Parnassia Beach Chair*, chair, 2007**
Moooi, beech, linnen, NP

***Shiitake*, stool, 2007**
Moroso, polyethylene, P

***Bella Barbara*, *Bella Beatrice*, *Bella Belinda*, *Bella Bettina*, *Bella Betty*, *Bella Brigitte*, *Big Ben Bianco*, hanglamp, 2007**
Personal Editions, polyester, painted NP (with the exception of *Big Ben Bianco*)

***Calvin*, floor lamp, 2007**
Personal Editions, polyester, fabric, P

***Chest of Boxes*, cabinet, 2007**
Personal Editions, glass, cardboard boxes, NP

***Crochet Courage*, dog sculpture (unique piece), 2007**
Personal Editions, crocheted rope secured with epoxy resin, sand blasted
Based on the design *Puppy* by Eerno Aarnio (2005), a toy

***Crochet Light*, floor lamp, 2007**
Personal Editions, crocheted rope secured with epoxy resin, sand blasted, NP

***Egg Vase Special*, Interpolis pattern, 2007**
Personal Editions, painted and glazed porcelain, gold leaf, NP

***Nosé Key Chain*, key chain, 2007**
Personal Editions, metal, precious metal coating, P

***Lucky One XL*, sculpture, 2007**
Personal Editions, polyester, NP

***Pizzo Carrara Bench and Table*, bench and table, 2007**
Personal Editions, marble, P

***Rainbow Necklace*, necklace, 2007**
Personal Editions, various beads, NP
Edition of 25

***Topiary: Bob, Frank, Mary, Sid*, objects, 2007**
Personal Editions, handmade cotton crochet, secured with epoxy resin, sand blasted, P

***Olympic Bowl: Triumph / Passion / Emotion*, bowls, 2007**
ceramic, NP
Commissioned by Randstad

tulip vase, 2007
porcelain, NP
Commissioned by Randstad

***Bacchus*, wine bottle rack, 2007**
Slide, polyethylene, P

***Chubby* and *Chubby Low*, chair and lounge chair, 2007**
Slide, polyethylene, P

***White Collection*, vase, stool, bowl, 2008**
B&B Italia, glazed ceramic, P

***Carmen*, wall tiles, 2008**
Bardelli, ceramic, P

***Iris 1* and *2*, wall tiles, 2008**
Bardelli, ceramic, P

***Minoo*, floor tiles, 2008**
Bardelli, ceramic, P

Christmas collection, 2008
De Bijenkorf, various materials, NP

***Antelope 2*, car (unique piece), 2008**
Bisazza, glass mosaic and various materials

***Aqua Jewels*, collection of taps, 2008**
Bonomi, chromed brass, P

***Tartan: Alastair, Ian, Kenneth, Tavish*, carpet tiles, 2008**
Colorline, chromojet print on different textiles, P

***Couture: Alice, Audrey, Grace, Henry, Isabella, Kelly, Stella, Suzanne*, wallpaper, 2008**
Graham & Brown, printed paper, NP

***Atmosphere*, seating, cushion, tables, 2008**
Kettal, various materials, NP

***KLM tablecloth* (Christmas gift), 2008**
cotton, viscose, NP
Commissioned by KLM

***Boutique Sofa*, sofa covers, 2008**
Moooi, textile, P

***Naval Brass Collection*: candle holders, tables, vase, plate, bowl, 2008**
Moooi, coated brass, NP

***Container*, bowl base, 2008**
Moooi, polyethylene, P

***Delft Blue Collection*, vases, 2008**
Moooi, painted and glazed ceramic, P

***Moooi Carpet Collection*, carpets, 2008**
Moooi, printed polyamide, P

***Bearbrick*, toy, 2008**
Personal Editions, plastic, NP

***Moosehead*, sculpture, 2008**
Personal Editions, ceramic or polyester, P

***Toast*, sculpture, 2008**
Personal Editions, various materials, P

***Tree of Life*, object, 2008**
Personal Editions, polyamide, NP

***Artus* (sofa), *Gentle* (cradle), *King and Queen* (bed), side tables, 2008**
Poliform, upholstered polyurethane, metal, NP

***World Tablecloth*, tablecloth, 2008**
cotton, viscose, NP
Commissioned by Randstad

***January Gift*, clock, 2008**
various materials, NP
Commissioned by Randstad

***Swarovski Crystal Palace: Aqua Jewels*, crystal shower and crystal mosaic, 2008**
Swarowski and Bisazza, chromed brass, Swarovski crystals, Bisazza crystal mosaic, NP

Led Candlelight, table lamp, 2009
Flos, Zamak, NP

Skygarden Recessed,
recessed ceiling lamp, 2009
Flos, aluminium, plaster, glass,
steel, P

Wallflower, lamp, 2009
Flos, aluminium, glass, P

Wattcher, energy meter, 2009
Innovaders, ABS, rubber, P

Parent Chair and *Table*,
chair and table, 2009
Moooi, expanded polypropylene
(EPP), P

Splinter Special: Black,
vase, 2009
Moooi, crystal glass, blown
and hand beaten, NP

The Killing of the Piggy Bank,
piggy bank, 2009
Moooi, glazed porcelain, P

Knotted Chair Special: Gold,
lounge chair, 2009
Personal Editions, knotted carbon
and aramide fibre cord, secured
with epoxy resin, sand blasted,
gilded, P

Wallflower Bouquet,
wall lamp, 2009
Personal Editions, wood,
polyester, aluminium, glass, NP

Senseo, coffee machine, 2009
Philips, various materials, NP

Venus, chair, 2009
Poliform, plastic, leather, metal
and integral polyurethane, P

Holiday Collection 2009, 2009
Target, various materials, NP

KDDI Phone, mobile phone
for IIDA (prototypes), 2010
Alessi, polycarbonate, embossed
and painted, and various
materials

*United Crystal Forest: Forest
of Dreams*, candlesticks, votive
holders, vases, 2010
Baccarat, partly cut crystal glass, NP

*United Crystal Forest: Woods
of Euphoria*, decanters, glasses,
2010
Baccarat, crystal glass, NP

*United Crystal Forest: Rois de
la forêt*, vases, 2010
Baccarat, cut crystal, metal,
marble, P

*United Crystal Forest: Spirits
of the Woods*, tall deer, medium
deer, small deer, floor candle
holders, 2010
Baccarat, crystal glass, metal, P

*United Crystal Forest Limited
Edition: One Minute 1, 2* and *3*
Baccarat, crystal, gold lustered
ceramic, NP

*United Crystal Forest Limited
Edition, plateau 1, block 2,
3* and *4*, champagne cooler,
vases, 2010
Baccarat, crystal, marble, NP

*United Crystal Forest Limited
Edition, Rois de la forêt vase*,
2010
Baccarat, crystal glass, NP

Drain Table, table, 2010
Cappellini, aluminium, NP

Flashback, chair, 2010
Cappellini, metal, reflecting
textile, NP

Tulip Chair, chair, 2010
Cappellini, metal, polyester,
textile, P

Jardin d'Eden, cutlery, trays
and underplate, 2010
Christofle, silver plated or
sterling, P

Collezione Privata, hair salon
furniture, 2010
Gamma & Bross, various
materials, NP

Vice & Virtue, perfume and
bottle, 2010
Cosme Decorte (Kosé), glass,
metal, NP

AQMW, make up and packaging
for skin care products, 2010
onwards
Cosme Decorte (Kosé), various
materials, P

Hero Pin, Pin, 2010
cardboard, metal, NP
Commissioned by Libelle

Make Up Collection, lipgloss,
lipstick, sheer mystery powder,
brush, brush clutch, false lashes,
concentrated scent, 2010
M.A.C., various materials, NP

Cyborg, chair, 2010
Magis, polycarbonate, P

Cyborg Wicker Club, Cozy
and *Elegant*, chair, 2010
Magis, polycarbonate, wicker, P

Sparkling Chair, chair, 2010
Magis, blow-moulded
polystyrene, P
Currently sold as *Still*

Troy Beech, chair, 2010
Magis, steel tube, plywood, P

*Boutique Cover: Eyes of
Strangers*, sofa cover, 2010
Moooi, polyester, cotton, linen, P

Boutique Sofa: Leather,
sofa, 2010
Moooi, steel, wood, upholstery,
leather, P

Container Table Skai, table,
2010
Moooi, mdf, skai, P

Fata Morgana TJ One and *Two*,
carpet, 2010
Moooi, printed polyamide, P

Monster Chair, chair, 2010
Moooi, steel, synthetic leather, P

Woood, table and desk, 2010
Moooi, beech, 3D pressed oak
veneer, P

Bon Bon Gold and *Bon Bon
Soilver*, lounge chairs, 2010
Personal Editions, knotted
aramide fibre cord with carbon
core, secured with epoxy resin,
gilded or silvered, P

Hairlamp, hanging lamp, 2010
Personal Editions, polyester, NP

Flex & Temp Workers Gift,
candle, 2010
wax, wick, NP
Commissioned by Randstad

Randstad Award, award, 2010
neodymium magnet, metal, P
Commissioned by Randstad

Impressions, flooring, 2010
Senso, biopolymers, P

Cinderella Broke a Leg,
bed, 2010
Skitsch, wood, polyurethane,
glass, iron, NP

Kelly, Stella and *Isabella,*
duvet covers, 2010
Skitsch, cotton, P (except for
Isabella)

One Nighter, sofabed, 2010
Skitsch, stainless steel, wood,
polyurethane, Swarovski buttons,
NP

Chubby Side Table,
side table, 2010
Slide, polyethylene, opal glass, P

Babel, chair, 2010
XO / Personal Editions,
polycarbonate, wood, P

Babel, tables, sofa, *Super Babel*
seating element (prototypes),
2010
XO, polycarbonate, wood

Eden, outdoor stool, outdoor
table, outdoor vase, 2010
XO, ceramic (stool),
polycarbonate, wood, NP

Pool table, 2011
Alcantara S.p.A., wood, alcantara, NP

Dressed, tableware collection
and glasses, 2011
Alessi, porcelain, stainless steel,
polished, crystal glass (glasses), P

Join, carpet, 2011
Anker Teppichboden, recycled
polyamide (aquafil econyl), tufted, P

*Embroidery, Decoupage,
Moonlight Garden, Daylight
Garden, Bloem, Tree,* wall tiles,
2011
Bisazza, glass mosaic, partly P

Big Shadow Special: Eyeshadow,
floor lamp, 2011
Cappellini, metal, ink jet printed
pvc and viscose fabric, P

*Saint-Jacques: Spinner 55,
Spinner 67, Spinner 76,*
suitcases, 2011
Fabbrica Pelletterie Milano, virgin
polycarbonate, P

Can Can and *Can Can Mini,*
hanging lamp, 2011
Flos, perspex, polycarbonate, P

Chrysalis, floor lamp, 2011
Flos, cocoon resin, steel, glass, P

Haiku, wall towl holder, vases,
toilet roll holders, toilet brush
holder, sponge and soap holder,
2011
Geesa, stainless steel, ceramics,
wood, P

*Whispers, Rosebeds, Key Muses,
Forest Muse, Braille Chester,*
2011
Graham & Brown, flocked paper, P

European and *World Business
Class Tableware,* in-flight
service, 2011-2013
various materials, P
Commissioned by KLM

Limited edition face powder, 2011
Cosme Decorte (Kosé),
crystal glass, metal, NP

Autumn/Winter 2011,
collection of products, 2011
Marks & Spencer, various
materials, NP

Crochet Light Special: Gold,
floor lamp, 2011
Personal Editions, crocheted gold
cotton rope, secured with epoxy
resin, sand blasted, gilded, P

Olympic Tin, tin, 2011
aluminium, NP
Commissioned by Randstad

Pause Mug, mug, 2011
ceramic, NP
Commissioned by Randstad

Star Tin, tin, 2011
aluminium, NP
Commissioned by Randstad

Typy, tent, 2011
Skitsch, aluminium, polyester, NP

Lipstick *Annelie, Annemiek,
Felicienne, Inez,* lipgloss *Jana,
Julia, Karin,* compact powder
Sheer Mystery Powder,
mascara, brush, perfume, 2012
M.A.C., various materials, NP

Dressed Pots & Pans Non Stick,
saucepan, casseroles, frying
pans with handles, deep frying
pan, 2012
Alessi, aluminium, stainless steel,
P

Fatman, folding etagere, 2012
Alessi, stainless steel, transfer, P

Marcel Wanders Collection,
duvet covers, bath towels and
accessories, 2012
Essenza, printed, cotton, P

Limited edition compact
powder, 2012
Cosme Decorte (Kosé), various
materials, NP

Troy polycarbonate and *Troy
on Wheels,* chair, 2012
Magis, steel tube, polycarbonate,
P

Spring/Summer 2012,
collection of products, 2012
Marks & Spencer, various
materials, NP

Autumn/Winter 2012,
collection of products, 2012
Marks & Spencer, various
materials, NP

Big Ben, clock, 2012
Moooi, fibreglass, powder coated
aluminium, P

Boutique Sofa, sofa covers,
2012
Moooi, wool, polyester, P

Container, chair and table, 2012
Moooi, polyethylene, P

Monster Barstool, barstool, 2012
Moooi, steel, synthetic leather, P

Valentine and *Valentine Baby*, hanging lamp, 2012
Moooi, glass, chromed, gold plated or lacquered metal, P

China Trends Award 2012, award, 2012
ceramic, NP
Commissioned by The Brand Partner

Dressed Pots & Pans: Aluminium, casserole, colander, large pot, pasta pot with drainer, 2013
Alessi, aluminium, P

Dressed: Watches, watches, 2013
Alessi, stainless steel, leather, P

Big New Antiques Vase, vase, 2013
Baccarat, full lead crystal, P

New Tile Collection, tiles, 2013
Bisazza, pressed ceramic, P

Dalia, armchair, 2013
Cappellini, fibreglass, resin, polyethurane foam, P

Deco Doors, door system, 2013
Cappellini, pressed wood (light oak or wenge), P

Saint-Jacques: New Colours, suitcases, 2013
FPM, polycarbonate, P

Bell Deco, limited edition face powder, 2013
Cosme Decorte (Kosé), painted and glazed ceramic, gold-plated metal, P

Christmas Coffret, skincare and make up products, 2013
Cosme Decorte (Kosé), various materials, P

Cyborg, chair, 2013
Magis, airmoulded polycarbonate, P

Troy, chair, 2013
Magis, steel tube chromed or painted in polyester powder and cataphoretically treated, polypropylene, also a version with upholstery, P

Spring/Summer and *Autumn/Winter 2013*, collection of products, 2013
Marks & Spencer, various materials, NP

Urbanhike, side table, 2013
Moooi, chromed steel, decalized aluminium wood transfer, P

Bell Lamp, hanging lamp and floor lamp, 2013
Moooi, glass, ceramic, metal, P

Zliq, sofa, 2013
Moooi, steel, foam, dacron, upholstery, different covers, P

Canvas Sofa, sofa, 2013
Moooi, steel, foam, dacron, upholstery, different covers, P

Cloud Sofa, sofa, 2013
Moooi, wood, foam and dacron, steel, different covers of different materials, P

Container New Antiques: Barstool, barstool, 2013
Moooi, polyethylene, P

Farooo Lamp, floor lamp, 2013
Moooi, polyethylene, P

Ink Airborne Chandelier, hanging lamp, 2013
Moooi, polycarbonate, chromed metal, P

Valentine Flat, hanging lamp, 2013
Moooi, glass, chromed, gold plated or lacquered shade, metal, P

Phoebe 1, floor lamp (unique piece), 2013
Personal Editions, carbon and aramide fibre cord, secured with epox resin, polyester, leds

Phoebe 2, floor lamp (unique piece), 2013
Personal Editions, polyether foam painted in an acrylic paint, spinnaker cloth, polyamide cotton, steel, leds

Phoebe 3, floor lamp (unique piece), 2013
Personal Editions, steel, spinnaker cloth, polyamide, cotton, leds

Phoebe 4, floor lamp (unique piece), 2013
Personal Editions, mohair weave, monofil, led lights, steel wire

Flat Marble Vases, objects, 2013
Personal Editions, onyx, gilded metal, NP

Carbon Balloon Chair and *Barstool*, chair and stool, 2013
Personal Editions, carbon fibre, blown and secured with epoxy resin, sand blasted, P

Mad Chair, chair, 2013
Poliform, moulded polyethurane, polyester, leather or fabric, wood, P

Flattering, hanging lamp, 2013
Moooi, metal wire frame, polycarbonate lenses, ultra thin suspension wire, P

Diamonds on Steroids, pouffe, 2013
Moooi, powdercoat ed steel, matrass, P

Dressed, breakfast collection, 2014
Alessi, various materials

Exceptional Items, clocks, candelabra, amphora, 2014
Christofle, silver or stainless steel

General Collection, nesting tables, chair, matryoshka, world globe, small tray, coffret, 2014
Christofle, silver or stainless steel

Glass Bench, bench, 2014
Personal Editions, sandblasted, tempered glass, cast iron

Snotty Vase XL, objects, 2014
Personal Editions, painted wood; polished bronze

One Minute Delft Blue Plate XL, plate and vase, 2014
Personal Editions, painted and glazed ceramic

3D Haikus, New Collection, decorative object, 2014
Personal Editions, polyamide, 3D printed with the SLS technique

Big Mask, object, 2014
Personal Editions, expanded polystyrene, airbrushed polyrea, steel

Think Collection, furniture collection, 2014
Yoo, wood, upholstered foam

Interior design

The year given refers to the year of completion. The year refers only to the date of the final design in the case of projects that were not executed.

design for exhibition about Emmy van Leersum, Museum Het Kruithuis, 's-Hertogenbosch, The Netherlands, 1992 (not executed)

design for exhibition 'De Oogst', in collaboration with Joost van Alfen, Stedelijk Museum, Amsterdam, The Netherlands, 1993

Canteen for Een Huis Voor De Gemeenschap, in cooperation with Jeanne van Heeswijk, Oud-Beijerland, The Netherlands, 1996

Pure Energy, installation for Maison de Bonneterie shops, The Netherlands, 1997

Holland In Vorm, pavilion in De Bijenkorf department store, Amstelveen, The Netherlands, 1999

Lunch Lounge, restaurant/showroom for Co van der Horst shop, Amstelveen, The Netherlands, 1999

Royal Wing Room, VIP Room Dutch Pavilion, Expo 2000, Hanover, Germany, 2000

Stonehouses, flex work office for Interpolis, Tilburg, The Netherlands, 2002

Wanderduck, Flagship Store for Mandarina Duck, London, Great Britain, 2002

JVC, architecture apartment building, Mexico City, Mexico, 2003 (not executed)

fair stand for The Wanders Collection for Bisazza, 100% Design, London, Great Britain, 2004

Lute Suites, boutique hotel, Ouderkerk aan de Amstel, The Netherlands, 2005

Blits, restaurant, Rotterdam, The Netherlands, 2005

Fifteen, restaurant, 2005, advice

Soap Stars, fair stand for The Wanders Collection for Bisazza, Salone Del Mobile, Milan, Italy, 2005

fire station Leidsche Rijn, Utrecht, The Netherlands, 2005

office space for housing corporation Kristal, Rijswijk, The Netherlands, 2006

The Hotel on Rivington / Thor, restaurant and bar in the hotel, New York, United States, 2007

Personal Editions exhibition, Salone Del Mobile (Fuori Salone), Milan, Italy, 2007

Parnassia aan Zee, meeting room, Bloemendaal, The Netherlands, 2007-2008

offices for Brandnew Design, Weesp, The Netherlands, 2007

Mondrian LA, hotel interior for Morgans Hotel Group, Los Angeles, United States, 2007 (not executed)

Mondrian Las Vegas, hotel interior for Morgans Hotel Group, Las Vegas, United States, 2007 (not executed)

Villa Amsterdam, private residence, Amsterdam, The Netherlands, 2008

Haryadi Residence, architecture and interior private residence, Jakarta, Indonesia, 2008 (not executed)

Mondrian South Beach Miami, hotel interior for Morgans Group, Miami, United States, 2008

Casa Son Vida, private residence, Son Vida, Mallorca, Spain, 2008

Oeuvre 1985 - 2013   Ingeborg de Roode assisted by Roos Hollander

Westerhuis, office space, Amsterdam, The Netherlands, 2008

'My House Of Dreams', fair stand for Poliform, Salone Del Mobile, Fuori Salone, Milan, Italy, 2008

Sanderson, hotel interior for Morgans Hotel Group, New York, United States, 2008 (not excuted)

showroom for Flos, Milan, Italy, 2008 (not executed)

'Daydreams', exhibition, Philadelphia Museum of Art, Philadelphia, United States, 2009

Villa Moda, multi-brand fashion store, Manama, Bahrain, 2009

reception area for employment agency Randstad, Groningen, The Netherlands, 2009

city planning and architecture for island Heart Of Europe, Dubai, United Arab Emirates, 2009 (not executed)

proposal Oudekerksplein, city planning, Amsterdam, 2009 (not executed)

Moët & Chandon, lounge for deparment store KaDeWe, Berlin, Germany, 2009 (not executed)

Kameha Grand Bonn Hotel, Bonn, Germany, 2010

Club Air, nightclub, Amsterdam, The Netherlands, 2010

mosaic for a swimming pool, private residence, Monaco, 2010

Yoo Cairo, business park, Cairo, Egypt, 2010 (not executed)

proposal Hotel Raamplein, Amsterdam, The Netherlands, 2010 (not executed)

Metcafé, café & kiosk in a shopping mall, Monaco, 2011

fairstand Euroshop 2011 for Anker Teppichboden, Düsseldorf, Germany, 2011

shop in shop concept for Kosé, several locations in Japan, from 2011

proposal Molen op de Kop / Java Eiland, landmark, Amsterdam, The Netherlands, 2011 (not executed)

proposal Georgia Landscaping, landscaping, Georgia, 2012 (not executed)

Andaz Amsterdam Prinsengracht Hotel, Amsterdam, The Netherlands, 2012

design for pitch Overhoeks Toren Hotel, Amsterdam, The Netherlands, 2012 (not executed)

Quasar Sales Center, Istanbul, Turkey, 2013

Mira Moon Hotel, Hong Kong, China, in cooperation with Yoo, 2013

Mondrian Doha Hotel for Morgans Group, Doha, Quatar, expected 2014

Kameha Bay Portals, resort, Mallorca, Spain, expected 2015

Kameha Grand Zürich Hotel, Zurich, Switzerland, expected 2015

Quasar luxury apartments, Istanbul, Turkey, expected 2015

private residence Taipei, Taiwan, expected 2015

private residence, France, execution unknown

Art direction

Since 2001, Marcel Wanders has been the art director of the label Moooi, of which he is co-founder and owner. In 2002, in conjunction with Dutch photographer Erwin Olaf, he began to make publicity photos for Moooi. Since then, Wanders has also acted as art director on publicity photos for other companies for which he designs, for magazine covers, events and so on. If Wanders is also closely involved with the photography, or created the graphic design, that is mentioned here.

Collection and catalogues, Moooi, 2001 onwards

Nosé, photography, 2002 onwards

Double portraits, Moooi, photography, in cooperation with Erwin Olaf, 2002-2006

Boutique Sofa, Moooi, photography, in cooperation with Edland Man, 2005

International Design Yearbook, Laurence King Publishers, design, 2005

presentation of Studio Collection and advertisements for the entire Lensvelt collection, Lensvelt, art direction, 2005

collection of electrical appliances, HE, photography, photos in cooperation with Maarten van Houten, 2006

Limited Edition magazine cover, *Wallpaper*, May 2007, design, 2007

Three Queens **(Christmas Collection 2008)**, Bijenkorf, photography, 2008

Aqua Jewels, Bonomi, photography, 2008

Couture, Graham & Brown, photography, 2008

Haikus, Moooi, photography, 2008

Still Life, Moooi, photography, in cooperation with Erwin Olaf, 2008

Superheroes, Moooi, photography, in cooperation with Erwin Olaf, 2008

Christmas collection and gift guide, Target, 2009

AQMW **Make Up**, Cosme Decorte (Kosé), collection and photography, photos in cooperation with Erwin Olaf, 2010 onwards

AQMW **Skincare**, Cosme Decorte (Kosé), collection and photography, photos in cooperation with Erwin Olaf, 2010 onwards

Vice & Virtue, Cosme Decorte (Kosé), perfume and photography, photos in cooperation with Erwin Olaf, 2010

Limited Edition Face Powder, Cosme Decorte (Kosé), photography, in cooperation with Erwin Olaf, 2010 onwards

World Class Service **and** *Business Class Service*, KLM, photography, 2010

Magazine cover *Libelle* **March 2010**, design, 2010

Cyborg, Magis, photography, 2010

Magazine cover *TL* **April-May-June**, design, 2010

Dressed, Alessi, photography, 2011

Dressed for the Occasion, Alessi, video installation, 2011

Join **catalogue**, Anker Teppichboden, 2011

Jardin d'Eden, Christofle, photography, 2011

Magazine cover *Corriere Della Sera* **12 April 2011**, design, 2011

Get Lit, Get Ink'd - Can Can Mini&Chysalis Launch Event, Flos, 2011

Can Can Mini&Chrysalis launch, Flos, 2011

Whispers, Graham & Brown, photography, 2011

Autumn / winter collection, Marks & Spencer, photography, 2011

Mermaids, Moooi, photography, 2011

Magazine cover *Oggetti Design Magazine* **August – September – October**, design, 2011

Dressed Pots & Pans, Alessi, photography, 2012

Fatman, Alessi, photography, 2012

United Crystal Forest, Baccarat, photography, 2012

The Wanders Collection Exhibition at Cersaie fair, Bologna, Bisazza, 2012

Big Shadow, Cappellini, photography, 2012

Marcel Wanders Collection, Essenza, photography, 2012

AQMW **Make Up** *Global Launch Event (at Moooi)*, Cosme Decorte (Kosé), 2012

Spring/Summer Collection, Marks & Spencer, photography, 2012

Autumn/Winter collection, Marks & Spencer, photography, 2012

Inside the Box, Moooi, photography, in cooperation with Erwin Olaf, 2012

Magazine cover *Time Out*, design, 2012

Dressed Pots & Pans: Aluminium, Alessi, photography, 2013

Spring/Summer collection, Marks & Spencer, photography, 2013

Autumn/Winter collection, Marks & Spencer, photography, 2013

Other projects

Vertelling van kinderen en badwater, story, 1985 (published in 1989, later available as diy booklet, downloadable from the website, and in 2001 published as simple booklet in English as *A Tale of Children and Bathwater*)
paper / digital, NP

Tijdschrift voor een snel vergetende wereld (edition of 1), magazine, 1987-1992
glass, metal, marble, gold leaf, NP

Chair Rabbit, photo, 1990
photoprint
As a postcard at Art Unlimited, NP

Baby announcement card, 1995
paper, luminescent material
Commissioned by Teake Bulstra (director of DMD)

Orange (Dance Cd), cd and booklet from the series *Couleur Locale for Oranienbaum*, 1999
Droog, polycarbonate, NP

Easter egg, 2004
Personal Editions / De Volkskrant, photoprint, NP

Corporate design, 2005
Commissioned by Co van der Horst

Fili Neri, Muchia Nera, Sussuro Nero, etchings, 2006
Personal Editions, magnesium etching, NP

Thor, art print, 2007
Personal Editions, print on canvas, NP

Mandarina Duck, art print, 2007
Personal Editions, print on canvas, NP

Big Shadow Milano and **Big Shadow New York**, art prints, 2007
Personal Editions, print on canvas, NP

Nosé, art print, 2007
Personal Editions, print on canvas, P

Death Is My Friend, art print, 2008
Personal Editions / Luminaire, print, NP

Superheroes: Angelita Angeleyes, Boom Boom Bitch, Tomoons, Twin Doctor, Bumper, Float Van Der Bilt, photographs, 2010
Lumas, lambda colour prints, glossy, P

Three Queens: Black Queen, White Queen, Gold Queen, photographs, 2010
Lumas, lambda colour photo prints, glossy, P

Christofle Jardin d'Eden Muses, engraved plates and prints, 2010
Personal Editions, engraved and polished rvs, prints, NP

Lingam, art print, 2010
Personal Editions, print, NP

Join, art work, 2011
Anker Teppichboden, dibond print, NP

Phoebe 4, video, 2013
Personal Editions, digital data, P
edition of 5

Virtual Interiors, German room, Wieliczka Salt Mine, Poland, digital video, 2011-2013
digital data, P

Virtual Interiors, Last Gypsfulvus' Room, Srinagar, India, digital video, 2011-2013
digital data, P

Virtual Interiors, Tilikums' Pool Tauranga, New Zealand, digital video, 2011-2013
digital data, P

Virtual Interiors, Cottonwood Spa, Cottonwood, USA, digital video, 2011-2013
digital data, P

Virtual Interiors, Smoking Room, Roswell, New Mexico, digital video, 2011-2013
digital data, P

Virtual Interiors, The Neighbors, Gulf of Aqaba, Saudi Arabia, digital video, 2011-2013
digital data, P

Virtual Interiors, Saakashvili Casino, Batumi, Georgia, digital video, 2011-2013
digital data, P

Virtual Interiors, Debauchery Room, Soyuz Centre, Kamchatka Krai, Russia, digital video, 2011-2013
digital data, P

Resumé

Education

1981–1982 Academy for Industrial Design Eindhoven (NL) (now Design Academy)

1982–1985 Maastricht Academy for Applied Arts (NL), jewellery department

1983–1985 Hasselt Academy of Fine Arts (BE)

1985–1988 Institute of the Arts, Arnhem (NL), department 3D Design, graduated cum laude

1995 Personal training by Richard Greene

1995 Course NEI (Neuro-Emotional Integration) therapist

1995–2001 Seminars at Anthony Robbins

2013–2014 MBA, Insead, Fontainebleau (FR)

Practice

1988 Working as an independent designer in Rotterdam (NL)

1989 Working as a teacher at various academies

1990–1992 Industrial designer at Landmark Design & Consult b.v., Rotterdam

1992 Establishment WAAC's Design & Consults together with three colleagues, Rotterdam (Wanders leaves in 1995)

1995 Working for some time as an NEI therapist

1995 Establishment design studio Wanders Wonders, Amsterdam (NL)

2000-2001 Project manager Vitra summer academy, Boisbuchet (FR)

2001 Establishment new design studio Marcel Wanders Studio, Amsterdam (now called Marcel Wanders)

2001 Establishment Moooi, Amsterdam together with Casper Vissers; the products that were produced under the name of Wanders Wonders go to this company of which Wanders becomes art director

2005–2011 Co-owner of Lute Suites, Ouderkerk aan de Amstel (NL)

2008 Development together with Aedes Real Estate of the Westerhuis, Amsterdam

2008 Partner in project development company Yoo, London (GB)

2011 Co-founder and board member of THNK, Amsterdam School for Creative Leadership

2012 Co-owner of Andaz Hotel, Amsterdam

2013 Establishment together with Paul Geertman of The Mind's Eye, a video art collection

Prizes and awards (selection)

1986 First prize design competition 'Olympic Design 8692' with a box with olive branch and a gold-coated plate (US)

1986 First prize design competition 'Café Modern' with *Dipstick*, Nestlé/Nescafé (NL)

1989 First prize design competition 'Verzamelband', Industrieel Ontwerpen and Albracht Systemen

1989 Start Stipend Ministry of Culture

1990 Third prize design competition 'Standing indoor lamp' with *Set Up Shades*, Amsterdam

1996 Kho Liang Ie encouragement Award for *Knotted Chair*, Amsterdam Fund for the Arts

1997 Audience award Rotterdam Design Prize for *Knotted Chair*

1998 Winner Woonbeurspin (NL)

1998 Honourable mention 'Compasso d'Oro' (IT)

2000 George Nelson Award, *Interiors Magazine* (US) Alterpoint Design Award 2000, Milan

2001 Technology Award for *Airborne Snotty Vases*, *Wired Magazine* (US)

2002 Man of the year, *MAN* (NL)

2003 Selected as one of Europe's 25 Leaders of Change, *BusinessWeek* (US)

2003 Elle Decoration International Design Award for *Patchwork Plates*

2003 Vredeman de Vries design award for *Patchwork Plates*

2003 *FX* International Interior Design Award 'best furniture or lighting for residential interiors' for Moooi collection

2004 Winner Löberschütz design competition with water bottle design and branding new brand Celsius, Munich (DE)

2005 Elle Decoration International Design Award for Carbon Chair, designed by Bertjan Pot in collaboration with Marcel Wanders

2006 Designer of the Year 2005, Elle Decoration International Design Award

2006 Designer of the Year, *Gioia Casa* (IT)

2006 Best interior professional for Moooi collection, Dutch Interior Awards (Sanoma)

2007 Visionary! Award, Museum of Arts and Design, New York

2007 Elle Decoration International Design Award for Skygarden

2009 Design Excellence Award, Collab, the Philadelphia Museum of Art's modern design collaborative

2009 Best Lounge/Bar for Mondrian South Beach Hotel, Miami, International Hotel/Motel Restaurant Show Gold Key Award (US)

2010 MIPIM Award category Hotels for Kameha Grand Bonn Hotel (GB/US)

2010 Best Business Hotel for Kameha Grand Bonn, Wallpaper (GB)

2010 International Property Award for Kameha Grand Bonn (GB)

2010 Winner ICT Environment Award for Wattcher (NL)

2011 Schlemmer Atlas Hotel of the Year for Kameha Grand Bonn, Busche Verlag, Dortmund

2011 Winner Japan Packaging Competition Award for *AQMW* collection (JP)

2011 Best consumer product Dutch Design Awards, for *Heracleum* for Moooi (design Bertjan Pot, technique Marcel Wanders)

2011 Hotel of the Year – worldwide for Kameha Grand Bonn, Diners Club Magazine Award (US)

2012 Winner iF Product Design Award for Haiku collection for Geesa (DE)

2013 Best Hotel Interior for Hotel Mira Moon, Asia Pacific Hotel Awards, Hong Kong

2013 Winner Best Leisure Architecture, Best Apartment and Best Development Multiple Units, for Quasar Residences Istanbul, International Property Awards (GB)

2013 Winner of the first prize in Best High-Rise Architecture, Best Leisure Development, Best Residential High-Rise Development and Best Mixed Use Architecture for Quasar Residences Istanbul, European Property Awards (GB)

2013 Best Commercial & Mixed Use Project (Future) for Quasar Residences Istanbul, Cityscape Global Awards

2013 Travel + Leisure Hotel of the Year 2014 for Andaz Hotel, GaultMillau (FR)

Exhibitions (selection)

1985 'Jewellery for the Head and Hair', Schmuckmuseum, Pforzheim (DE)

1986 'Café Modern', Gallery Association Designers, Leeuwarden (NL), and travelling

1986 'Le Vent du Nord III', Institut Néerlandais, Paris (FR)

1986-1987 'Jewellery / Images' travelling exhibition on the occasion of 10 years VES

1987 Solo 'Marcel Wanders', Gallery Marzee, Nijmegen (NL)

1988 'Le Vent du Nord', Institut Néerlandais, Paris

1989 'New Designers, ioN foundation, Rotterdam

1989 'Umbrella - Parasol', Gallery Coumans, Utrecht (NL)

1989 'Combs', Gallery Marzee, Nijmegen (NL), and travelling

1989 'The Enlightenment', Gallery Puntgaaf, Groningen (NL)

1990 'Prototype', Gallery Kapelhuis, Amersfoort (NL)

1990 'The Embarrassment of riches', EEG congress, Avignon (FR)

1991 Presentation: 'And on the eighth day men started to lie' in de Kunstpassage, The Hague (NL)

1992 'Material, Fabric for Design', Stedelijk Museum, Amsterdam

1992 'Dutch Design', Institut Teknologi Bandung, Bandung (ID)

1992 'Furniture Sculpture', Commanderie of St. Jan, Nijmegen

1993 'An art collection of combs', Mikimoto, Ginza, Tokyo (JP)

1993 'Made in Holland', Museum für angewandte Kunst, Cologne (DE)

1993 'Droog Design, selection of Dutch design', Pastoe showroom, Fuori Salone (presentation outside the fair during Salone Internazionale del Mobile), Milan (IT)

1995 'Mentalities', Securitas Gallery, Bremen (DE), and travelling

1995 'Mutant Materials in contemporary design', MoMA, New York (US), and travelling, in 1997 Groninger Museum, Groningen

1995-1996 'Droog Design. Retrospective', Kunsthal, Rotterdam

1996 'Rotterdam Design Award', Kunsthal, Rotterdam

1996 'Scanning', Stedelijk Museum, Amsterdam

1996 'Thresholds. Contemporary Design from the Netherlands', MoMA, New York

1996 'Plastics New Treat', Droog Design, Fuori Salone, Internos Gallery, Milan

1997 'Dry Tech II' and 'Droog for Rosenthal', Droog Design, Fuori Salone, Milan

1997 'The Ecology Series 1 Glamour', Material ConneXion, New York

1997 'AVA Ceramics Award', Princessehof, Leeuwarden (NL)

1997 'Droog Design', Design Museum, Helsinki (FI)

1997 'Droog Design. Contemporary Design from the Netherlands', Kulturbrauerei, Gallery im Pferdestall, Berlin (DE)

1997 'Materials in Design', international travelling exhibition (Centraal Museum, Utrecht, and Tekniska Mässan, Stockholm (SE) amongst others)

1997 'Architecture and Design in the Netherlands', Stilwerk Design Center, Hamburg (DE)

1997 'Droog Design 1991-1996', Centraal Museum, Utrecht (international travelling exhibition)

1997 'Rotterdam Design Award, Kunsthal, Rotterdam

1998 'Double Dutch - Essentials de Luxe', Centro Cultural de Belem, Lisbon (PT)

1998 'Material innovation gallery', Material ConneXion, New York

1998 'The Inevitable Ornament', Droog Design, Spazio Solferino, Fuori Salone, Milan

1999 'Good Goods', MMKA, Arnhem (NL)

1999 Solo 'Wanders Wonders. Design for a New Age', Museum for Modern Art Het Kruithuis, 's-Hertogenbosch (NL)

1999 'Couleur Locale for Oranienbaum', Droog Design, Spazio La Posteria, Fuori Salone, Milan

1999 Solo 'Wanders Wonders', Frederieke Taylor | TZ'Art Gallery, New York

1999 'Design Manifestation 2', Museum Waterland, Purmerend (NL)

1999 'Vase for the occasion', Museum for Modern Art Het Kruithuis, 's-Hertogenbosch (NL)

2000 'Hitec-Lotec', travelling exhibition (GB)

2000 'Droog & Dutch Design', Living Design Centre Ozone, Tokyo (JP)

2000 Solo 'Wanders Wanted', Material ConneXion, New York

2000 'Design World', Design Museum, Helsinki (FI)

2000 'Droog Design. Dutch design for the nineties and beyond', Israel Museum, Palevsky Design Pavilion, Jerusalem (IL)

2000 Presentation in Limn, San Francisco (US)

2000 'Van A tot Zit', Stedelijk Museum Roermond (NL)

2001 'Can of Gold', Gallery Xprssns, Hamburg (and later in other cities)

2000 'Droog Design', Trapholt Museum, Kolding (DK)

2000 'The new Chain of Function', Stedelijk Museum, Amsterdam

2000 'Via Milano', Society Baby, Amsterdam

2002 '21 diadems for Máxima', Museum for Modern Art Het Kruithuis, 's-Hertogenbosch (NL)

2002 'Home made Holland', Crafts Council, London

2002 'Body Design', San Francisco Museum of Modern Art (SFMoMA)

2002 'Strangely Familiar: Design and Everyday Life', Walker Art Centre, Minneapolis (US)

Resumé

2002 'Skin: Surface, Substance + Design', Cooper-Hewitt Museum, New York

2002 'Via Milano. New Dutch Design', Society Baby, Amsterdam

2002 'Milan in a Van', Victoria & Albert Museum, London

2002 'River Deep, Mountain High', Het Glazen Huis, Amsterdam

2002 'Prototypes', Museum Waterland, Purmerend (NL), and travelling

2002 'Celebrating Dutch Design', Apartment Zero, Washington (US)

2003 'Via Milano. New Dutch Design', Interior design fair RAI, Amsterdam

2003 'The Origin of Things', Museum Boijmans van Beuningen, Rotterdam

2003 'Swarovski Crystal Palace', Fuori Salone, Milan

2003 'Your choice', Droog Design, Galleria Postart, Fuori Salone, Milan

2003 'Reality Machines', Netherlands Architecture Institute (NAi), Rotterdam, and travelling

2003 'Tafelplezier', Museum for Modern Art Het Kruithuis, 's-Hertogenbosch (NL)

2004 'Simply Droog', Haus der Kunst, Munich, and travelling

2004 'Armour, the fortification of man', Fort Asperen, Acquoy (NL)

2004 Presentation in Design Lab Nike, Portland (US)

2004 'Kramer vs. Rietveld. Contrasts in the furniture collection', Stedelijk Museum CS, Amsterdam

2004 'Observatory on the Spread of Creativity', Museo d'Arte Contemporanea Villa Croce, Genoa (IT)

2004 'Via Milano 04. New Dutch Design', RAI, Amsterdam

2004 'Designers Present', MU, Eindhoven (NL)

2004 'The foreign affairs of Dutch Design', BNO, travelling exhibition

2004-2005 'Metallic Yellow - Gold for Robert Smit', Stedelijk Museum CS, Amsterdam

2005 'Touch me', V&A, London

2005 'Nest. Designs for the interior', Stedelijk Museum, Amsterdam

2005 'Dutch at the Edge of Design. Fashion and Textiles from the Netherlands', Museum at FIT, New York

2006 'Droog Material', Centraal Museum, Utrecht (NL)

2006 'NLA. Netherlands to Los Angeles', ACME Gallery, Los Angeles (US)

2007 Presentation in Dundee Contemporary Arts, Dundee (GB)

2008 'Pretty Dutch', Princessehof, Leeuwarden (NL)

2009 Solo 'Daydreams', Philadelphia Museum of Art (US)

2010 'Exposition Collective', Arums Gallery, Paris

2013 'Hand Made - Long Live Crafts', Museum Boijmans van Beuningen, Rotterdam

2013 'Stedelijk Museum Amsterdam presents Marcel Wanders and Benthem Crouwel', Capital Museum, Beijing (CN)

2013 'Salon/Lace', Museum Het Grachtenhuis, Amsterdam

2014 'Marcel Wanders: Pinned Up at the Stedelijk. 25 Years of Design', Stedelijk Museum Amsterdam

Bibliography

P. Antonelli, *Thresholds. Contemporary Design from the Netherlands*, New York 1996 (exh. cat. New York – MoMA)

P. Antonelli, *Ron Arad. No Discipline*, New York 2009 (exh. cat. New York – MoMA)

P. Antonelli and Y. Joris, *Wanders Wonders. Design for a New Age*, 's-Hertogenbosch/Rotterdam 1999 (exh. cat. 's-Hertogenbosch – Het Kruithuis)

W. Benjamin, *The Arcades Project*, Cambridge, MA/London 1999. Translated by H. Eiland and K. McLaughlin

W. Benjamin, 'Louis Philippe or the Interior', reprinted in C. Briganti and K. Mezei (eds.), *The Domestic Space Reader*, Toronto 2012

O. Bennett, 'The Wonder of Wanders. The Dutch Designer Marcel Wanders is Flying High', *The Sunday Times*, 25 January 2009

T. Benton, *The Modernist Home*, London 2006

J. Bernard, *Letters on the English and French Nations; Containing Curious and Useful Observations on their Constitutions Natural and Political*, London 1747

A. Betsky and A. Eeuwens, *False Flat. Why Dutch Design is So Good*, London 2004

B. Bettelheim, *The Uses of Enchantment. The Meaning and Importance of Fairy Tales*, New York 1976

W. Bettens, 'Wanders Revisited', *DAMn magazine* (2009) 21, 25-32

A. Beukers and E. van Hinte, *Lightness. The Inevitable Renaissance of Minimum Energy Structures*, Rotterdam 1998

D. Biersteker, 'Operatie Lute. Een nieuw hotelconcept langs de Amstel', *Het Parool*, 3 December 2004

F. Böhm, *KGID. Konstantin Grcic Industrial Design*, London 2005

L. Bossi, 'Nella città di Amsterdam, le bandiere rosse di una citadella creativa, nata da un'idea di Marcel Wanders, designer radicato nella tradizione / In Amsterdam, red flags on a creative citadel signal an idea realised by Marcel Wanders, a designer rooted in tradition', *Domus* (2010) 943, 98-103

P. Bourdieu, *Distinction. A Social Critique of the Judgement of Taste*, London/New York 1984

D. Bradbury, 'Marcel Wanders. Casa Son Vida / Mallorca, Spain, 2009', *The Iconic Interior. 1900 to Present*, London 2012, 326-329

Y. Brentjens, 'Terug naar de zwier van paraplu en parasol', *Het Financieele Dagblad*, 10 and 12 June 1989

Y. Brentjens, 'Wilde haren in een wrong', *Het Financieele Dagblad*, 18 May 2001

R.F. Broekman and O. Winkler, 'Different Personalities. Ralf F. Broekman and Olaf Winkler in Conversation with Marcel Wanders', *Build* (2010) 1, 41-47

J. Brouwer, A. Mulder and L. Spuybroek (eds.), *The Politics of the Impure*, Rotterdam 2010

P. Bruyn, 'De emancipatie van het Sieraad', *NRC Handelsblad*, 4 April 1986

P. Buchanan et al., *Soeters van Eldonk Architecten. Dialoog met mensen en plekken*, Amsterdam 2008

M.E. Bucquoye and A. Beukers, *Van bakeliet tot composiet. Design met nieuwe materialen / From Bakelite to Composite. Design in New Materials*, Oostkamp 2002

P. Bueters, 'Wanders' wereld', *FEM Business & Finance* (2009) 22 August, cover, 24-40

M. Byars et al., *50 Chairs. Innovations in Design and Materials*, Crans-Près-Céligny n.d. [1997]

M. Byars et al., *New Chairs. Design, Technology, and Materials*, London 2006

S. Caan, *Rethinking Design and Interiors. Human Beings in the Built Environment*, London 2011

S. Calatroni, 'Destroy and Create,' *Interni* (1996) 463, 181

L. Carroll, *Alice's Adventures in Wonderland*, 1865

M. Castelein, 'Wanders Wonders. Design voor nu en later', *Eye. Zicht op trends* (1999) December, 10-11

N. Chiam, 'Wanders Struck', *Female* (2012) September, 242-245

L. Choi, 'Marcel Wanders', http://www.designboom.com/interviews/marcel-wanders-designboom-interview, 16 December 2004

L. Coirier, 'Marcel Wanders. Design is the World', *TL Magazine* (2010) 6, 28-31

L. Coirier, 'Marcel Wanders & Erwin Olaf. The Dream Team', *TL Magazine* (2011) 10, 74-79

B. Colomina, *Privacy and Publicity. Modern Architecture as Mass Media*, Cambridge, MA 1994

W. Crouwel and H. Steenbruggen, *Swip Stolk. Master Forever*, Groningen 2000

J. Dalton, 'Boy Wanders', *Financial Times*, 12 April 2003

J. Dalton, 'A lesson in job satisfaction. Colossal, controversial and with a challenging beauty,

Studio Job's creations have the longevity of fine art', *Financial Times*, 20 October 2007

I. de Roode, 'Spannende dromen. Van massaproduct tot designobject', *Het Financieele Dagblad*, 3 April 1999

I. de Roode, 'Bertjan Pot', *Stedelijk Museum Bulletin* (2005) 1, 30-32

I. de Roode, 'Industriële vormgeving / Industrial Design', in: *Aanwinsten / Acquisitions 1993-2003 Stedelijk Museum Amsterdam*, Amsterdam 2006, 98-105

I. de Roode, 'I want to make new things. Innovation in the work of Ron Arad', in: P. Antonelli, *Ron Arad. No Discipline*, New York 2009, 11-25 (exh. cat. New York – MoMA)

I. de Roode, 'Form Follows Function? 150 Years of Furniture Design', *Stedelijk Collection Reflections: Reflections on the Collection of the Stedelijk Museum Amsterdam*, Amsterdam/ Rotterdam 2012, 313-332

I. de Roode, 'Altes Handwerk und niederländische Designer der Gegenwart / Oude ambachten en hedendaagse Nederlandse ontwerpers,' in: N. Uniquole (ed.), *Dutch Design. Exzellentes Handwerk am Hofe / Uitmuntend ambacht aan het hof*, Dessau 2012, 160-162

F. de Wild, 'Middle East Motifs. Villa Moda Bahrain Mixes the Design Language of Marcel Wanders with the Skills of Regional Artisans,' *Frame* (2009) 69, 82-90

E. de Wolfe, *The House in Good Taste*, New York 1913

L. den Besten, 'Geheim verbond. Oesters & zwijnen, Besems & Wanders', *Bijvoorbeeld* (1995) 1, 25-29

L. den Besten, 'In de knoop zitten', *Het Parool*, 31 December 1996

L. den Besten, 'Marcel Wanders: "ik ben niet geïnteresseerd in onzindingetjes"', *Bulletin Fonds voor beeldende kunsten, vormgeving en bouwkunst* (1997) October, 15-18

L. den Besten, *De nieuwe keten van de burgemeester. Een verslag van de werkgroep ambtsketen*, Amsterdam 2001

L. den Besten, *Sense of Wonder. Chi ha paura...?*, 's-Hertogenbosch 2002 (exh. cat. Het Kruithuis)

L. den Besten, 'Van lauwerkrans tot helm', *Vitrine* (2002) 5, 46-49

L. den Besten, 'Meestbesproken meubel op de beurs in Milaan. Een kroonluchter met engel die vriendelijk de champagne schenkt', *Trouw*, 23 April 2005

L. den Besten, 'Digitale foto's in de vorm van honderd tegels op de muur of als print op de vloer', *Trouw*, 18 June 2005

exh. cat. *Design in Nederland*, The Hague (Nederlandse Kunststichting) 1981, travelling exhibition

C. Dickens, *Hard Times [1854]. An Authoritative Text, Backgrounds, Sources, and Contemporary Criticism* (G. Ford and S. Monod, eds.), New York 1966

M. Dings and J. Schilder, 'Fraaie spruitjes. De kwaliteit van Nederlands design', *De Tijd* (1988) 11 November, 28-33

T. Dixon, 'The Ten Best Chairs', *The Independent*, 1 May 2002

L.A. Dosi Delfini, *The Furniture Collection Stedelijk Museum Amsterdam, 1850-2000. From Michael Thonet to Marcel Wanders*, Amsterdam 2004

M. Douglas, 'Bad Taste in Furnishing', in: *Thought Styles. Critical Essays on Good Taste*, London 1996

P. Doze, 'Space M. Wanders', *Intramuros* (2002) 102, 70-77

exh. cat. *Dutch Form. Materiaal, stof voor vormgeving*, Amsterdam (Stedelijk Museum) 1992

L. Edelkoort, *Armour*, Paris 2003 (exh. cat. Acquoy – Fort Asperen)

P.H. Eek et al. (eds.), *Boek. Piet Hein Eek 1990-2006*, Eindhoven 2006

T. Eliëns, *Kunstnijverheid of industriële vormgeving. Dat is de kwestie*, Zwolle 1997

T. Eliëns et al., *21 Diademen voor Máxima /21 Tiaras for Máxima*, 's-Hertogenbosch 2002 (exh. cat. 's-Hertogenbosch – Het Kruithuis)

T. Eliëns, *Bořek Šípek. Glas, design, architectuur*, Zwolle 2006

H. Erkelens and R. Koster, *Vredeman de Vries Prijs voor vormgeving 2003. 20 Nominaties*, n.p. [Leeuwarden] 2003 (exh. cat. Franeker – Museum 't Coopmanshûs)

R. Erven, 'Reflecteren op geschiedenis', *De Architect interieur* 36 (May 2005) 17, 22-25

A. Eschbach, '"Wir verkaufen Träume statt Polster." Marcel Wanders macht Design mit mehr als einer Prise Humor', *Neue Zürcher Zeitung*, 23 April 2006

E. Escher, 'De grote decoratiegolf', *Elsevier* (2005) October, Thema Interieur, 21-23

E. Escher, '"Ik ben dol op die prachtige arrogantie van Dutch designers". Interview met Paola Antonelli, designconservator bij het MoMA in New York', *Elsevier* (2007) April, Thema Interieur, 28-31

exh. cat. *Studio Joris Laarman. Stranger than Fiction*, Burgos (Centro de Arte Caja de Burgos) 2008

K.J. Fielding, 'Charles Dickens and the Department of Practical Art', *The Modern Language Review* XLVIII (1953), 270-277

F. Fisher, T. Keeble, P. Lara-Betancourt and B. Martin (eds.), *Performance, Fashion and the Modern Interior*, London 2011

B. Fitoussi and A. Betsky, Richard Hutten. *Works in Use = For You*, Oostkamp 2006

P. Freriks, 'Frisse noordenwind waait in Parijs op designgebied', *De Volkskrant*, 1 October 1986

A. Friedman, *Woman and the Making of the Modern House. A Social and Architectural History*, New Haven/London 2006

K. Ganfield, 'Marcel Wanders', *Soma* 27 (2013) 1, 52-57

G. Gibson, 'Rooms with New Views. Andaz in Amsterdam by Marcel Wanders', *Frame* (2013) 91, 116-117

S. Giedion, *Space, Time and Architecture*, Cambridge, MA 1941

E. Goedegebuure, 'Wanders Wonders!', *Eigen Huis & Interieur* (1998) July, 22-23

'Gold für die Dose', *Arcade* (2001) 6, 38

A. Goldwasser, 'Natural Wanders', *ID-magazine* (2000) March/April, 80-85

M. Haas, 'Marcel Wanders. De Hotte Ontwerper', *Nieuwe Revu* (1999) January, 28

L. Hales, 'Our House is No Longer Bauhaus at MoMA', *The Wall Street Journal Europe*, 19-21 November 2004

P. Hall, 'Dutch designer Marcel Wanders Attempts to Apply his Midas Touch to the World of Retail', *Metropolis* (2003), February, 76-81

W.P. Hartman, 'Gezinsgewijs sinteren', *Product* (2001) September, 38-40

S. Heerma van Voss, 'De vrienden van Wanders. "Onze cultuur lijdt aan een verheerlijking van het jonge"', *NRC Handelsblad*

D. Hell (ed.), 'Ontwerper met commercieel instinct', *Adformatie*, 24 (1996) 43, 17

T. Hendriks, ' Man van het Jaar 2002: Marcel Wanders. Interview van het Jaar', *Man* (2003) 1, 38-42

'Hogeschool voor Beeldende Kunsten, Arnhem. Lamp en fauteuil', in: exh. cat. *Nieuwe ontwerpers. Een greep uit het afstudeerwerk van 1988*, Rotterdam (Stichting ioN) 1989

M. Horsham, 'What is Droog?', *Blueprint* (1996) October, 3-6

C. Hospes, 'Mooi, mooier, moooi', *HP|De Tijd*, 19 September 2003

C. Hospes, 'Moooi in Milaan', *De Volkskrant*, 3 April 2004

J. Hudson, 'Refining and Redefining', *Canadian Interiors* 41 (2004) 1, 30-32

F. Hufnagl, *Plastics + Design*, Stuttgart 1997 (exh. cat. Darmstadt – Museum Künstlerkolonie Mathildenhöhe)

J. Huisman, 'Designridders tussen droom en daad', *De Volkskrant*, 31 October 1992

J. Huisman, *Vaas voor de gelegenheid*, 's-Hertogenbosch 1999 (exh. cat. Museum Het Kruithuis – 's-Hertogenbosch)

J.V. Iovine, 'The Retro and the Restless. Two Milans', *The New York Times*, 17 April 1997

M. Janssen, 'Marcel Wanders maakt cadeaus voor de wereld', *Libelle* (2010) 10, 26-33 (special edition with Wanders as art-director)

G. Jeffers, 'The Eighth Wanders', *Surface Magazine* (2001) 31, 146-150

E. Jinek, 'Marcel Wanders. Het beste komt nog', *De Telegraaf*, 2 February 2013

W. Jones, 'The Wandering Marcel', *Elemente* 4 (2009) 1, cover, 74-87

J. Junte, 'Design met volume. 'Voormalig stofzuigerfabrikant' HE maakt de blits met ontwerpen van Marcel Wanders', *De Volkskrant*, 3 December 2005

R. Kaal, 'Zeldzaam duur. Een tafel van 127.000 euro? Geen punt. Nu kunst en fotografie (bijna) onbetaalbaar zijn geworden, komt voor beleggers een nieuw terrein in beeld: design', *HP|De Tijd* (2007) 22 June

D. Kaufman, 'Wanders Lust. A Major U.S. Retrospective Celebrates the Dutch Design Genius', *TIME Magazine* 175 (2010) 6, 50-51

J.A.J. Kemps, *AVA Keramiek Award 1997*, Leeuwarden 1997

G. Kennedy, 'Behind the Ceiling', http://www.design.nl , 27 May 2009

K. Kleinman, J. Merwood-Salisbury and L. Weinthal (eds.), *After Taste. Expanded Practice in Interior Design*, New York 2012

A. Koch (ed.), *Galerie Kapelhuis. Dertig jaar vernieuwing in de toegepaste kunst 1960-1990*, Rotterdam 2003

R. Koelewijn, 'Lunchen met Marcel Wanders. "Als businessman ben ik een *amateur*"', *NRC Handelsblad*, 12 October 2013, L8-L9.

H. Kool, 'Het individuele koffiedrinken overtuigend aangepakt en opgelost', *NRC Handelsblad*, 22 March 1986

R. Kras and G. Waldmann, 'Institutioneel ontwerpen', in: G. Staal and H. Wolters (eds.), *Holland in vorm. Vormgeving in Nederland 1945-1987*, The Hague 1987 (exh. cat. Amsterdam – Stedelijk Museum)

C. Kruit, 'De uitdaging van de tijd', *Detail in architectuur* (2000) June, 13

K. Kuijpers, 'Wanders wandelt niet, hij rent', *Algemeen Dagblad*, 28 February 2009

Le Corbusier, *Vers une architecture*, Paris 1923. Translated by John Goodman as *Toward an Architecture*, Los Angeles 2007

A. Leclaire, 'Marcel Wanders. Meer is meer', *Vrij Nederland* 74 (2013) 15, 68-73

S. Levy, 'Go BIG or Go Home. When it Comes to Decor, Are You a Neo-Surrealist Technophile or Handicraft Lover? Milan's Annual Salone Proves Everything Goes', *The Globe and Mail*, 5 May 2007

Bibliography

B. Lootsma, *Bijlage bij het diploma van Marcel Wanders behaald aan de Hogeschool voor de Kunsten Arnhem, afdeling 3D-design*, 1988 (typescript)

S. Lovell, *Limited Edition. Prototypen, Unikate und Design-Art-Möbel*, Basel/Boston/Berlin 2009

C. Lucassen, 'Contacten, design, cappucino en wijn in Milaan', *Het Financieele Dagblad*, 17 April 2004

G. Lueg (ed.), *Made in Holland. Design aus den Niederlanden*, Tübingen/Berlin, 1994 (exh. cat. Cologne – Museum für Angewandte Kunst Köln)

E. Lupton, *Skin. Surface, Substance + Design*, New York 2002 (exh. cat. New York – Cooper Hewitt Museum)

B. Maandag, 'De veelzijdige wereld van de industriële vormgevers. Jonge ontwerpers exposeren bij Stichting ioN', *Rotterdams Nieuwsblad*, 19 January 1989

'Marcel Wanders. Dipstick', flyer Stichting Vormgever, 29 April 1987

'Marcel Wanders. Product Designer, Moooi', *BusinessWeek* (2002) 17 June, 56

M. Margetts, *Tord Boontje*, New York 2006

F. Massoni, 'Wonderful Wanders', *Oggetti Design Magazine* (2011) 3, 104-111

'Maxima's kroon', *Materialise Vandaag*, (2002) 2, 6

S. McKellar and P. Sparke, *Interior Design and Identity*, Manchester 2004

E. Melet, 'Ingebouwde oudheid', *De Architect* (1998) January, 71

exh. cat. *Meubelsculptuur. Wonderlijke tafels en stoelen... of beeldhouwwerken?*, Nijmegen (Nijmeegs Museum Commanderie van St. Jan/Galerie Marzee) 1992

R. Craig Miller, 'Neo-Decorative Design', in: R. Craig Miller, P. Sparke and C. McDermott, *European Design Since 1985. Shaping the New Century*, London/New York 2008, 226-253

R. Craig Miller, P. Sparke and C. McDermott, *European Design Since 1985. Shaping the New Century*, London/New York 2008

'Mobili europei. Artifort', *Domus* (1987) 685, n.pag.

'Mobilis. Marcel Wanders', *MD* (1987) 6, 46

S. Moreno, *Marcel Wanders. Behind the Ceiling*, Berlin 2009

A. Myzeley and J. Potvin (eds.), *Fashion, Interior design and the Contours of Modern Identity*, London 2010

M. Ogundehin, 'Droog Design's dry wit', *Blueprint* (1994) September, 51

'Ontwerpen als marathon', *Rotterdams Nieuwsblad*, 27 October 1990

'De oogst', *Bijvoorbeeld* 25 (1993) 2+3, n.pag. [65] (exh. cat. Amsterdam – Stedelijk Museum)

M. Ouwendijk, 'Vier ontwerpen voor een nieuw KLM-servies', *Bijvoorbeeld* (1989) 4, 22-23

M. Philippa et al., *Etymologisch Woordenboek van het Nederlands*, Amsterdam 2003-2009

S. Philippi, *S+arck*, Cologne 2003

E.A. Poe, 'Philosophy of Furniture', in: *The Complete Tales and Poems of Edgar Allan Poe*, Harmondsworth 1984 (1840)

'Qualified Design in Like a Well Trained Salesman, Wanderswonders' (text in Japanese), *Monthly Design* (1999) September, 138-141

B. Radice, *Memphis. Research, Experiences, Results, Failures and Successes of New Design*, London 1985

R. Ramakers and G. Bakker, *Droog Design. Spirit of the Nineties*, Rotterdam 1998

R. Ramakers and G. Bakker (eds.), *Couleur Locale. Droog Design for/für Oranienbaum*, Amsterdam/Rotterdam 1999 (exh. cat. Milan - Salone del Mobile / Fuori Salone - and Oranienbaum – Schloss Oranienbaum)

R. Ramakers, *Less + More. Droog Design in Context*, Rotterdam 2002

R. Ramakers, 'Geen minachting', *Items* (2005) 4, 13

R. Ramakers (ed.), *Droog. A Human Touch*, Amsterdam 2006

A. Rawsthorn, 'Milan's Surreal, Supersized Creations. Products, and Ideas, Were Bigger than Life at the Furniture Fair', *International Herald Tribune*, 23 April 2007

C. Reinewald, 'Voorzichtig! Breekbaar. Nieuw Nederlands gebruikskeramiek', *Items* (1993) 1, 32-37

A. Ribbens, '"Met een kleine ambitie kom je nergens." Industrieel vormgever Marcel Wanders wil spelend de dingen veranderen', *NRC Handelsblad*, 24 July 2003

A. Ribbens, 'Design voor keuken en badkamer', *NRC Handelsblad*, 24 January 2006

C. Rice, *The Emergence of the Interior. Architecture, Modernity, Domesticity*, London 2006

E. Rodrigo, 'Design als Notwendigkeit. Die Rolle der Behörden', in: G. Lueg, *Made in Holland. Design aus den Niederlanden*, Cologne/Tübingen/Berlin 1994

V. Rosner, *Modernism and the Architecture of Private Life*, New York 2005

exh. cat. *Rotterdam Design Prize 1997 / Designprijs Rotterdam 1997*, Rotterdam (Kunsthal) 1997

'Salone del mobile 2009. Moooi,' *Eigen huis & interieur* (2009) September, 230-231

J. Scelfo, 'Marcel Wanders on Designing Upbeat Tableware', *The New York Times*, 16 March 2011

K. Sharma, 'Marcel Wanders. Design Can Change a Throwaway Society', *Livemint.com*, 13 February 2013

R.G. Saisselin, *The Rule of Reason and the Ruses of the Heart. A Philosophical Dictionary of Classical French Criticism, Critics and Aesthetic Issues*, Cleveland/London 1970

H. Schmidt, *Behind the Seen. Studio Dumbar*, Mainz 1996

L. Schouwenberg, 'New Nostalgia,' *Frame* (2002) 25, 106-109

L. Schouwenberg, 'A Dutch Perspective on Craft,' in: *The Future is Handmade. The Survival and Innovation of Crafts*, The Hague 2002, 108-121

C. Seite, 'Linoleum. Design over de vloer,' *Het Financieele Dagblad*, 1 February 2006

R. Sennett, *The Craftsman*, London 2008

M. Sevil, 'Marcel Wanders ziet alles anders', *Het Parool*, 9 December 2006

J. Smeets and N. Tynagel, *The Book of Job*, New York 2010

P. Sparke, *Elsie de Wolfe. The Birth of Modern Interior Decoration*, New York 2005

P. Sparke, *The Modern Interior*, London 2008

P. Sparke, A. Massey, T. Keeble and B. Martin (eds.), *Designing the Modern Interior. From the Victorians to Today*, London 2009

P. Sparke, *The Jungle in the Parlour*, forthcoming

N. Spönhoff, 'Marcel Wanders, een veelbelovende jonge ontwerper,' *Items* 8 (1988) 27, cover, 18-21

G. Staal, 'Toegepaste kunst', in: *Scanning. Toegepaste kunst en fotografie in Amsterdam 1996*, Amsterdam, n.pag. (exh. cat. Amsterdam – Stedelijk Museum))

G. Staal, 'Salone del Mobile Milaan. Geen namen maar ideeën', *Vormberichten* (1996) May, 14

G. Staal, *Double Dutch*, Lisbon 1999 (exh. cat. Lisbon – Centro Cultural de Belém)

G. Staal, 'De export van een paradijs. Nederlandse vormgeving in het buitenland,' *More than Tulips. Kwartaaltijdschrift van de Vereniging voor Internationale Culturele Betrekkingen* 1 (1998) March, first issue, 7-9

I. Start, 'New Yorkers zijn dol op onze ontwerpen', *Elsevier* (2013) 37, 56-57

Stedelijk Collection Highlights. 150 Artists from the Collection of the Stedelijk Museum Amsterdam, Amsterdam 2011, 189

exh. cat. *Studio Joris Laarman. Stranger than Fiction*, Burgos (Centro de Arte Caja de Burgos) 2008

N. Swengley, 'High Style from the Low lands', *Financial Times*, 20-21 October 2007

J. Szita, 'Little Gem. Like a Fabergé Egg, or Indeed Like a City Itself, Marcel Wanders' First Completed Residential Project in Amsterdam Is Small But Exuberantly Formed', *Frame* (2009) 68

T. te Duits, *The Origins of Things. Sketches, Models, Prototypes*, Rotterdam 2003 (exh. cat. Rotterdam – Museum Boijmans van Beuningen)

J. Temmen, 'Marcel Wanders', *Schöner Wohnen*, May 2013, 143-146

P. ter Hofstede (ed.), *Memphis 1981-1988*, Groningen 1989

P. Terreehorst, 'Sportuitzet voor Amsterdamse bruid', *De Volkskrant*, 11 October 1986

R. Thiemann, 'Spinner of Tales', *Frame* (2000) 17, 40-47

R. Thiemann, 'Staging Spaces', in: M. Wanders et al., *Marcel Wanders. Interiors*, New York 2011, 4-5

L. Tischler, 'Moooi fabulous', *Fast Company* (2008) 129, 107-113

A. Tölke, 'Darf's ein bisschen mehr sein? Designer Marcel Wanders und die neue Üppigkeit', *Der Standard (Rondo)*, 21 September 2012, 12-14

M. Unger, 'VES. Het ontstaan van een reizende tentoonstelling', *Bijvoorbeeld* (1985) November, 34-36

T. van den Boomen, 'Hightech-macramé', *Intermediair* 33 (1997) 11, 37

M. van Dodewaard, 'Marcel Wanders. Doen maar vooral ook denken', *Mari* (1999) June, 110-116

M. van Eeuwen, 'Een innovatieve uitslover', *NRC Handelsblad*, 3 July 2002

M. van Empel, 'Marcel Wanders. Eigenlijk wil ik alles', *Woonbeeld* (1990) 1, 8-11

J. van Heeswijk and E. Luermans (eds.), *Een huis voor de gemeenschap Oud-Beijerland 1995-2003*, Amsterdam 2003

W. van Herwijnen and M. Wanders (eds.), *Amsterdam Creative Capital. Highlights of an Ongoing Creative History*, Amsterdam 2009

E. van Hinte, *Ed Annink. Designer*, Rotterdam 2002

A. van Galen, 'Paraplu-project van Leni Coumans inspireert tot kunstzinnige noviteiten van vormgevers', *Utrechts Nieuwsblad*, 30 May 1989

P. van Kester, 'Perfectie met pietluttigheid. "Docent terrible" Dick Lion (Arnhem)', *Items*, (1999) 4, 68-69

B. van Lier, 'Producten voor de eeuwigheid. Eternally Yours strijdt tegen de verspilling van massaproductie', *Adformatie* (1997) 33/34, 36-38

B. van Lier, 'Nederlandse ontwerpers over hun buitenlandse escapades. "Design is gewoon business"', *Items* (2004) 3, 48-51

I. van der Linden, 'Hightech materialen, lowtech esthetiek', *Decorum* 15 (1997) 4, 35-37

B. van Mechelen, 'Renny Ramakers over Droog Design', *Items* (2004) 6, 40-45

B. van Mechelen, 'Marcel Wanders. Grow More Fish', *Items* (2005) 1, 27

L. van der Post, 'A Wanders-Full World', *Financial Times*, 6 February 2010, cover, 8-12

R. van Tilborg, 'Geen vormgeving maar vormvinding', *Identity Matters* (2003) May, 76-81

J. van Uffelen, 'Het ik-tijdperk in de koffie. Boxtelnaar Marcel Wanders wint prijs met de Dipstick', *Brabants Dagblad*, 22 March 1986

V. van de Vliet, 'Moooi, zo'n snotvaas', *Het Parool*, 7 April 2001

M. van Zalingen, 'Breien en knopen met high-tech vezels', *Eigen Huis & Interieur* 29 (1996) 11, 12-13

M. van Zalingen, 'Het EH&I estafette-interview. Jan des Bouvrie & Marcel Wanders', *Eigen Huis & Interieur* 34 (2001) 2, 55-57

M. van Zalingen, 'Het EH&I estafette-interview. Marcel Wanders / Lidewij Edelkoort', *Eigen Huis & Interieur* 34 (2001) 3, 31-35

I. van Zijl, *Droog Design 1991-1996*, Utrecht 1997

I. van Zijl, 'Marcel Wanders', *Droog & Dutch Design. From Product to Fashion: The Collection of the Centraal Museum*, Utrecht 2000, 168-171 (exh. cat. Tokyo – Living Design Center Ozone)

J. Veldkamp, 'Dutch Design staat stil', *Elsevier* (2003) October, Thema Interieur, 65-68

L. Verweij, 'Dutch design: niet meer dan een geslaagde brandingstrategie. Socioloog Werner Sewing over Nederlands ontwerp,' *Items* (2005) 3, 64-66

N. Vinson, 'Moooi. Man's Dream Comes True', *Financial Times*, 25 March 2006

N. Vinson, 'Marcel Wanders. Crochet Chair', *Financial Times*, 14-15 April 2007

Vivant Denon, *Point de lendemain suivi de Jean-François de Bastide, La Petite Maison*, (M. Delon, ed.), Paris 1995

M. Vlemmings, 'Kinderwagen Bugaboo en productielijn Moooi zijn grote internationale successen van eigen bodem', *Items* (2007) 6, pp

R. Voight, 'New Amsterdam. Fashion and Home Design Are Going Dutch', *The New York Times*, supplement, February 1999, 72-78

Voltaire, *Le Temple du Goût. Édition Critique par E. Carcassonne*. Lille 19532

R. Vuijsje, 'Ontwerper Marcel Wanders. "Een stoel gaat niet over zitten"', *Dagblad De Pers*, 5 December 2008

B. Walrecht, *Home Made Holland. How Craft and Design Mix*, London 2002 (exh. cat. London – Crafts Council Gallery)

'Wanders VIP-room. Himmel über Hannover', *Items* (2000) 5, 14

M. Wanders, 'Vertelling van kinderen en badwater' (1985), *De vierde Dimensie. Bulletin voor de afdeling 3D Design* 1 (1989) 1, 31-33

M. Wanders, 'Grow more fish', *International Design Yearbook* 20, London 2005

M. Wanders, 'Foreword. The Contemporary Renaissance of Humanism', in: M. Fairs, *21st Century Design. New Design Icons from Mass-Market to Avant-garde*, London 2006

M. Wanders, 'Wereld van Wanders. "Als ontwerper ben je een hofnar," *IN*, Winter 2009, 51

M. Wanders et al., *Marcel Wanders. Interiors*, New York 2011

M. Warner, *From the Beast to the Blonde. On Fairy Tales and their Tellers*, London 1994

I. Weyel, 'Dutch hotel design', *Het Financieele Dagblad*, 20 February 2010

I. Weyel, 'Wanders Wonderland', *NRC Handelsblad*, 27-28 October 2012

C. Wilk (ed.), *Modernism. Designing a New World 1914-1939*, London 2006 (exh. cat. London – Victoria and Albert Museum)

G. Williams, 'Global/Local', *Blueprint* (1999) June, 27

G. Williams, 'Working Wanders', *Design Week*, (2002) 1 February, 17-19

G. Williams, *The Furniture Machine. Furniture since 1990*, London 2006 (exh. cat. London – Victoria and Albert Museum)

G. Williams, *Telling Tales*, London 2009 (exh. cat. London – Victoria and Albert Museum)

L. Young, 'Making a Statement with "Mutant" Materials', *New York Times*, 24 April 1996 and *International Herald Tribune*, 27 April 1996

J.D. Zipes, *Fairy Tales and the Art of Subversion. The Classical Genre for Children and the Process of Civilization*, New York 1983

Index

3D Haiku 21, 105, 201, 206
3D printing 90, 105, 114
Aalto, Alvar 118
Abitare il Tempo, Verona 124
Academy for Applied Arts, Maastricht 14, 210
Academy for Industrial Design Eindhoven 14, 122, 210
Academy of Fine Arts, Hasselt 14, 210
ACME Gallery, Los Angeles 213
Aedes Real Estate 141, 210
Airborne Snotty Vase 21, 37, 90-91, 198, 211
Albracht Systemen 194, 210
Alessi 10, 28, 30, 170-171, 199, 203-205, 208
Alessi, Alberto 10
Alice in Wonderland 27, 43-44
Alfen, Joost van 16-17, 206
Alferink, Joost 16-17
Amsterdam Fund for the Arts, Amsterdam 122, 211
Andaz Amsterdam Prinsengracht, Hotel, Amsterdam 43-45, 98-101, 141, 207, 210-211, 216
Annink, Ed 13, 219
Antonelli, Paola 9, 19, 214-216
Apartment Zero, Washington 213
AQMW 152-153, 203, 208, 211
Arad, Ron 25, 31, 214-215, 218, 223
archetype 20, 42, 43, 59, 63, 73, 89, 157
Architecture Institute, Netherlands, Rotterdam 213
art, see: visual art
art direction 29, 30, 64, 73, 77, 84, 142, 156, 170, 175, 181, 207
ArtEZ, Arnhem 14
Artifort 14-16, 194, 217
Arts and Crafts movement 41-42
Arums Gallery, Paris 213
autonomous 13, 31
Baby, Society, Amsterdam 212-213
B&B Italia 29, 200-202
Baas, Maarten 29, 35, 178
Babel Chair 173, 204
baby-face fixation 20, 59
Bad Black Box 15, 194
Bakker, Gijs 16-17, 131, 194
Bär + Knell 20-21
baroque, Baroque 43, 85
Bastide, Jean François de 35-36, 219
Bauhaus 13, 40, 216
beauty 33, 40, 64
Belem, Centro Cultural de, Lisbon 212, 218

bells 31, 43, 83
Bells –
    Bell Deco 153, 205
    Bell Lamp 27, 205
    Bella Bettina 27, 179, 202
    Giant Bells 21, 154, 179
Benjamin, Walter 51-52, 54-55, 185, 214
Berkenbosch, Carolien 131
Besems, Dinie 130-131, 195, 215
Beukers, Adriaan 118, 121, 214
Beumer, Guus 10
Bey, Jurgen 16-17, 29-30
Big Ben Bianco 154, 202
Big Shadow Special: Eyeshadow 76-77, 204
Bisazza 23, 79, 106-107, 109, 158, 199-200, 202-206, 208
Blits, Restaurant, Rotterdam 42, 51-53, 206, 216
B.L.O. 20, 28, 157, 198, 201
BNO 213
Boffi 107, 197
Boijmans van Beuningen, Museum, Rotterdam 213, 218
Bonekamp, Lucas 7
Boontje, Tord 23, 217
Bottoni 24, 113, 199
Breakfast of a Dwarf Rabbit 74-75, 196
Breuer, Marcel 6, 162
Caan, Shashi 39, 214
Cacharel 137, 196
Calvin-lamp 27, 159, 202
Can of Gold 71, 198, 212
Capital Museum, Beijing 213
Cappellini 10, 18-19, 28-29, 34, 61, 76-77, 87, 105, 119, 125, 172, 195-198, 200-201, 203-205, 208
Carbon Balloon Chair 11, 19, 63, 162-167, 205
Carbon Chair, 25-27 164, 199, 211
Carbon Copy, 25-26 164
Card Case, 19, 23, 74 195
Casa Son Vida, Mallorca 43, 184, 206, 214
Castiglioni, Achille 19, 86
Centraal Museum, Utrecht 212, 213, 219
Chi Ha Paura...? 30, 58, 180, 196, 198, 215
Christe, Dienand 16-17
concept, conceptual 17, 21, 24
Cooper-Hewitt National Design Museum, New York 212
Coray, Hans 162

Corona de Agua 168, 198
Cosme Decorte 27, 137, 152-153, 203-205, 208
Crafts, handcrafted, craftsmanship 9, 14, 24, 26, 42, 43, 45, 73, 118, 121, 149
Crafts Council, London 212, 219
Crochet Table 25-26, 35-36, 132, 198
Couleur Locale for Oranienbaum 72-73, 196-197, 209
Coumans, Gallery, Utrecht 194, 211, 219
Couple vase 21, 103, 195
Couture, 84-85 202, 208
Craig Miller, R. 9, 22, 217
Crochet –
    Chair 25-26, 132, 201, 219
    Courage 132, 202
    Light 132, 202, 204
    Table 25-26, 35-36, 132, 198
customisation 24
Cyborg 27, 30, 142, 203, 205, 208
Wicker, 142, 203
dark, darker side 21, 47, 93, 192
Death is my Friend 192, 209
decoration 23, 24, 33-35, 42, 47, 54, 61, 95, 110
Delft Blue series 67, 96-97, 136, 154, 169, 179, 201, 202, 206
Delft Blue 67, 96, 99
Design Academy, Eindhoven 14, 122, 210
design fundamentalism 61, 87
Design Lab Nike, Portland 213
Design Museum, Helsinki 212
dialogues 20, 46, 103
Dickens, Charles, 34-35, 215-216
Dipstick 15, 29, 31, 66, 194, 210, 217, 219
Dixon, Tom 122, 215
DMD 17, 194-197, 209
Double Portraits 30, 113, 132, 155, 208
dream, dreams 9, 16, 93, 182
Dressed – 28, 30, 170-171, 204, 208
    for the Occasion 208
    Pots & Pans 205-206, 208, 170
Droog Design 16-18, 28-29, 118, 121, 212-213, 217-218, 219
Dry Tech 18, 21, 118, 212
Dudok van Heel, Menno 7
Dumbar, Gert 13
Dundee Contemporary Art, Dundee 213
durability 18, 19, 47
Dutch Design 17, 70
Dutch East India Company 45

Index

Dutch Minimalism 13
Eames, Charles & Ray 26, 118
Edelkoort, Li 19, 215, 222
Eek, Piet Hein 20, 21, 215
Egg Vase 27, 42, 60, 144-145, 196, 199, 202
Eindhoven, City of 197
Ephese 15, 194
Eurocarbon 118
European and World Business Class Tableware 156, 204
Expo 2000 42, 174, 197, 206
fairy-tale 42
fantasy 46
Farnsworth, Edith 34-35
Fishnet Chair 125, 198
Flare-table 24, 149, 200
Flos 18-20, 36, 57, 86, 104, 157, 198, 200-204, 207-208
Flying Knotted Chair 124-125, 201
Flying Table 81, 200
Fort Asperen, Acquoy 213, 215
Frederieke Taylor| TZ'Art Gallery, New York 212
functionalism, functionalist, functionality 13, 24, 58
Gaudí, Antoni 120-121
Geertman, Paul 141, 210
Gehry, Frank 162
Gilst, Karin van 6-7
Glass Bench 143, 205
Glazen Huis, Het, Amsterdam 213
Graham & Brown 84-85, 202, 204, 208
Grcic, Konstantin 20, 214
Greene, Richard 210
Geesa 204, 211
Grachtenhuis, het, Amsterdam 213
Groot, Marjan 11, 23, 32-37, 223
haiku 21, 45, 63
Haiku Collection 211
Happy Hour Chandelier 29-30, 201
Haus der Kunst, Munich 213
Hayon, Jaime 29, 44, 46
HE 116-117, 202
Heracleum 211
high tech (low tech) 118, 121, 142
Hogendijk, Martijn 118
Hoff, Dick van 17, 121
Hollander, Roos 3, 7, 193, 222
Hond, Iris 92
Horst, Co van der 28, 172, 206, 209
Hotel on Rivington, The, New York 29, 43, 166, 177, 207, 210
Hudson, Jennifer 11, 21, 38-49, 216, 223
humanising, humanism, humanist 24, 26, 40, 62, 117, 133
humour 28
Hutten, Richard 17, 20, 141, 216
Impressions 178, 204

Indianapolis Museum of Art 9
Innovaders 112, 203
innovation 25, 111, 117, 118, 157
Inside the Box 22, 29, 210
Institut Néerlandais, Paris 211
Institute of the Arts, Arnhem 14, 210
Institut Teknologi Bandung 212
Internos Gallery, Milan 212
Interpolis 23, 90, 110, 145, 198, 201-202, 206
ioN, Foundation 19, 194, 216, 217
Israel Museum, Jerusalem 212
Iwanicka, Barbara 7
Jongerius, Hella 17, 118, 122, 125
Jouin, Patrick 6
JVC, apartment complex, Mexico City 27, 206
Kameha Grand Bonn Hotel, Bonn 43, 82-83, 207, 211
Kapelhuis, Gallery, Amersfoort 103, 212, 217
Kartell 20, 201
Killing of the Piggy Bank vase 36-37, 203
KLM 16-17, 57-58, 156, 194-196, 202, 204, 208, 217
Knotted Chair 10-11, 18-19, 23, 25-26, 59-61, 118-125, 162, 164, 167, 172, 196, 198, 201, 203, 211
Knotted Table 125, 198
Konings, Jan 16-17
Koninklijke Tichelaar, Makkum 61, 63, 94-95, 103, 199
Koons, Jeff 167
Kosé 137, 153, 203-205-208
KPN 70, 201
Kruithuis, Museum het, 's-Hertogenbosch 59, 168, 197-198, 206, 212-216
Kunsthal, Rotterdam 212, 216
Kunstpassage, 's-Gravenhage 212
Laarman, Joris 25, 216
Lace Table 21, 23, 25, 132, 196
Lady Gaga 10
Landmark Design & Consult 15-16, 156, 195, 210
Le Corbusier 40-41, 217
Learoyd, Richard 71
Lensvelt B.V. 29, 200, 208
Lensvelt, Hans 29
lies 62-63, 131
Linning, Nanine 29-30
Lion, Dick 14, 219
Lippincott, J. Gordon 39
Lloyd Wright, Frank 51
Lovegrove, Ross 29
low tech 27, 118, 121
Lucy, 23 111, 174, 197
Lute Suites, Ouderkerk aan de Amstel 42-43, 61-62, 106-107, 141, 206, 210
Lijstbroches 24, 25

Magis 27, 30, 64, 80, 142, 197, 199-201, 204-205, 208
Mandarina Duck 25, 41, 43, 108, 115, 198, 206, 208
Marcel Wanders by Puma Collection 87, 201
Marcel Wanders Studio 210
Marks & Spencer 26-27, 203-205, 208
Marzee, Gallery, Nijmegen 21, 195-196, 211, 216
Material ConneXion, New York 212
Máxima, HRH Princess 168, 212, 215, 217
Meda, Alberto 27, 121, 164
Memphis 13-14, 17, 44, 217-218
Mies van der Rohe, Ludwig 34-35
Mikimoto, Ginza, Tokyo 212
Mind's Eye, the 210
minimalism 41
Mira Moon, Hotel, Hong Kong 207, 211
Mobilis 14-15, 194, 217
modernism, modernist 13, 20, 24, 34-35, 40, 41, 55, 61, 62, 95, 162
Molen op de Kop 88-89, 207
Mondrian Doha Hotel, Qatar 45, 47, 207
Mondrian South Beach Hotel, Miami 42, 44, 47, 51, 53-54, 146-147, 206, 211
Monster Chair 21, 79, 93, 204
Moooi 10-11, 18-19, 22-31, 33, 35-36, 45, 57-58, 60, 67, 74, 78, 93, 113, 132, 141, 144, 155, 164, 194-208, 211, 216-219
Moosehead 141, 169, 203
Morgans Hotel Group 47, 147, 206-207
Moroso 81, 200, 202
Morrison, Jasper 29, 35, 172
Murano Bags 108, 198
Museo d'Arte Contemporanea Villa Croce, Genua 213
Museum at FIT, New York 213
Museum für Angewandte Kunst, Cologne 212, 217
Museum of Modern Art, New York 212
MVRDV 29, 155, 174
narrative 20, 21, 30, 63, 64, 158, 182
Nescafé 66, 194, 210
Nestlé 14-15, 66, 210
New Antiques 19, 29, 45, 60-61, 87, 173, 176-177, 200-201, 205
Newson, Marc 31
Netherlands Foundation for Visual Arts, Design and Architecture 118
New Institute, The, Rotterdam 10
Nieuwenborg, Frans van 13
Ninaber van Eyben, Bruno 13
Nomad Carpet 28, 172, 196
Nosé(-portrait) 30, 158, 180-181, 200
Noten, Ted 168

Olaf, Erwin 22, 27, 29-30, 67, 113, 132, 145, 155, 207-208, 214, 215
Onderwater, Alexandra 11, 14, 56-66, 223
One Minute Sculptures, *One Minutes* 31, 133, 169, 200
Organon 16, 195
ornament, see: decoration
Osko + Deichmann 29
Ozone, Living Design Center, Tokyo 212, 219
Panton, Verner 6
Pastoe 212
Patchwork 21, 63, 94-95, 199, 211
Pearl Necklace 130-131, 195
Personal Editions 31, 37, 63, 71, 75, 90, 96, 105, 119, 124-125, 133, 136-139, 143, 154, 158, 163, 169, 179, 182-183, 192, 196-209
Pferdestal, Gallery im, Berlin 212
Phoebe 182-183, 205, 209
Pipe 107, 197
Pizzo Carrara Bench 31, 143, 202
Poe, Edgar Allan 33, 217
Poliform, 159, 200, 202, 205
Ponti, Gio 162
Portman, John 51
Postart, Gallery, Milan 213
postmodernism, postmodernist, postmodern 13, 14, 19, 41, 55, 62
Pot, Bertjan 22-23, 25, 26, 29, 164, 199, 211, 215
Princessehof, Museum het, Leeuwarden 212-213
Print 81, 200
Puma 87, 201
Puntgaaf, Gallery, Groningen 211
Putman, Andrée 46-47, 147
Quasar, apartment complex, Istanbul 45, 48, 126-127, 184, 207, 211
RAI Interior design fair, Amsterdam 213
Rainbow Necklace 29, 57, 158, 202
Ramakers, Renny 16-19, 22, 70, 121, 217-219
Random Light 22-23
recycling 20
Remy, Tejo 17
Rietveld, Gerrit 6, 213
Rivington, *The Hotel on*, New York 29, 42, 51, 176-177, 206
Roode, Ingeborg de 8-31, 42-43, 118-125, 162-167, 193-209, 215, 223
Rosenthal, Droog for 78, 144-145, 196, 212
Royal Wing Room, Expo 2000, Hannover 155, 174, 206
Salone del Mobile Milan, 206-207, 217-218
San Francisco Museum of Modern Art 212

scale 27, 39, 42, 45, 55, 77, 79, 80, 83
Schmuckmuseum, Pforzheim 211
Securitas Gallery, Bremen 212
Sennett, Richard 26-27, 218
Senso 15, 42, 178, 204
Set Up Shades 16-17, 19-20, 70, 194, 196, 210
Šípek, Borek 13-14, 215
skin, see: surface
Skygarden 36-37, 57, 104, 201, 203, 211
SLS 3D printing 25, 90
SLS Vase 25, 114, 197
Snow White 29
Soapbath Series, *The Wanders Collection* 79, 200
Soeters, Sjoerd 13
Sottsass, Ettore 13
Sparke, Penny 9, 11, 22, 50-55, 217-218, 212
Sparkling Chair 19, 80, 164, 203
Spazio Solferino, Milan 212
Sponge Vase 19, 24, 60, 78, 196, 199
St. Jan, Commanderie of, Nijmegen 212, 217
Stam, Mart 162
Starck, Philippe 10, 13-14, 30-31, 46-47, 147
Stedelijk Museum Amsterdam 13, 18, 21-22, 26, 121, 125, 131, 162, 206, 212-213, 215, 218-219
Stedelijk Museum Roermond 212
Stichting Kunst en Bedrijf 74, 195
Stilwerk Design Center, Hamburg 212
Still 80, 203
Stone Chair 23, 105, 198
Stonehouses 23, 110, 206
Stolk, Swip 13, 215
story, see - narrative
Studio Job 23, 29, 31, 44, 46, 49, 57, 215
surface (skin) 23, 55, 63, 92, 105, 133, 170
sustainability 13, 16, 18, 27, 40, 185
Swarovski 23, 109, 199, 202-204, 213
Swarovski Crystal Palace 23, 109, 203, 213
Tates, Sophie 7
Tape Necklace 75, 196
Tattoo 92
Target 26-27, 203, 208
taste 23, 33-37, 53-55, 61
Technische Universiteit Delft 18, 118
Tegenbosch, Pietje 11, 184, 185, 223
Tekniska Mässan, Stockholm 212
Textielmuseum, Netherlands, Tilburg 125, 174, 198
theater, theatrical, 26, 29, 34, 37, 42, 47, 51, 55, 57
Thiemann, Robert 9, 11, 14, 21, 47, 56-61, 125, 219, 223

THNK, Amsterdam School for Creative Leadership 210
Thonet, Michael 162, 166, 173, 215
Thor, restaurant, *The Hotel on Rivington,* New York 29, 43, 176-177, 206
Tichelaar, Koninklijke, Makkum 14, 15, 21, 61, 63, 94-95, 103, 194-195, 199
Topiaries 25-26, 138-139
Trapholt Museum, Kolding 212
Tulips 102, 195
United Crystal Forest 160-161, 203, 208
Urquiola, Patricia 20
variations 24, 70, 121
VES 14-15, 194, 211, 219
Vice & Virtue 137, 203, 207
Victoria and Albert Museum 9, 21, 213, 222, 223
Villa, The 87, 201
Villa Amsterdam, Amsterdam 45, 134-135, 206
Villa Moda, Manama, Bahrein 33, 45-46, 148-149, 207
VIP Chair 28-29, 155, 174, 197
visual art 31, 39, 46, 47, 184-185
Virtual Interiors 11, 31, 49, 184-185, 209
Vissers, Casper 29, 210
Vissers Design 29
Voltaire 36-37, 219
WAACs, WAAC's 16-17, 102, 210
Walker Art Center, Minneapolis 213
Wanderduck, London 115, 206
Wanders Wonders 16, 18-19, 23-24, 31, 59, 74-75, 120, 196-198, 210, 212, 214-216
Wanders Collection Soapbath Series 79, 200
Wanders Wonders Lighting 23-24, 196-197
Wandschappen 122-123
War on Design 19, 87
Waterland, Museum, Purmerend 212, 213
Wattcher 24, 112, 203, 211
Wax, 77 196-197
Wegman, Martijn 13
Westerhuis, Amsterdam 45, 57, 140-141, 178, 210
Wezel, Rudolf van 7
Willem-Alexander, HRH Prince 168
Williams, Gareth 9, 73
Willow Chair 72, 197
Wolfe, Elsie de 53-54, 218, 22, 223
Wunderkammer 45
WVC, Ministerie van 210
Xprssns, Gallery, Hamburg 212
Yoo, 206 210
Zeppelin 18-19, 86, 149, 200
Zupanc, Nika 29

About the Authors

Ingeborg de Roode studied History of Art at the University of Leiden. Since 2001 she is the curator for industrial design in the Stedelijk Museum Amsterdam. She has organised many temporary exhibits on design and, for the reopening of the Stedelijk Museum in 2012 she co-curated the much-praised design collection. She has published on GDR design, the cooperation between designers and industry, the application of new materials and technology (e.g. 'I want to make new things, Innovation in the work of Ron Arad' in exh.cat. of Centre Pompidou and MoMA, 2008/2009), international furniture design (e.g. 'Form Follows Function? 150 years of furniture design', in *Stedelijk Collection Reflections*, 2012) and other subjects. Her current research is on furniture design in the Amsterdam School Period and contemporary international industrial design.

Marjan Groot is senior lecturer in Design and Decorative Art Studies at the University of Leiden in the Netherlands. She received her doctorate on *Women Designers in the Netherlands 1880-1940*. Her research concerns all forms of design and decorative art, with a special focus on modernism and postmodernism. She aims to combine historical knowledge of design and decorative art with contemporary theoretical viewpoints. Recent publications include an edited volume on *Design and Gender* (2011) and a paper on 'Design, Gender and Biotechnology' (2013).

Educated at the Courtauld Institute of Art, **Jennifer Hudson** was the editor of the *International Design Yearbook* for over ten years, until it ceased publication in 2007. She is a regular contributor to industry magazines and journals and is the author of titles including: *1000 New Designs and Where to Find Them* (editions 1 & 2); *Interior Architecture Now; Process: Fifty Product Designs from Concept to Manufacture; Interior Architecture from Brief to Build and Architecture from Commission to Construction*. She is currently living and working in Ecuador.

Penny Sparke is Professor of Design History at Kingston University, London. Between 1982 and 1999 she taught on, and subsequently led, the History of Design programme run by London's Royal College of Art and Victoria and Albert Museum. Her best-known publications include *An Introduction to Design & Culture, 1900 to the present*; *As Long As It's Pink: The Sexual Politics of Taste*; *Italian Design*; *Japanese Design*; and, most recently, *Elsie de Wolfe: The Birth of Modern Interior Decoration and The Modern Interior*. She has also curated a number of exhibitions and broadcast widely on her specialist area.

Educated as a chemical engineer, **Robert Thiemann** soon became a copywriter and eventually journalist. He specialized in design, with a strong focus on interiors. In 1997 he co-founded *Frame: The Great Indoors*, an international bi-monthly magazine of interior design of which he still is editor in chief, and Frame Publishers. The company started to issue books on interior design in 2001. In 2005 Robert co-founded *Mark, Another Architecture*, a bi-monthly magazine about architecture, of which he was editor in chief until 2010. In 2009 Frame Publishers launched the art and visual culture magazine *Elephant*. Robert is one of two shareholders of Frame Publishers and the company's managing director.

Alexandra Onderwater graduated in Clinical Psychology in 2002. Taking only a backpack, she spent a year exploring in Southeast Asia; on her return, she followed the post-doc in Journalism (PDOJ) at Erasmus University, Rotterdam. Alexandra's interest in design and art, coupled with her international aspirations led her to *Frame*, where she holds both staff and freelance positions as (contributing) editor. Her freelance activities range from print (*Wallpaper, Mark*) to projects for creative agencies (Sid Lee, Staat), copywriting for designers and acting as moderator during the IDFA documentary film festival. She has made numerous *Wallpaper City Guides* (Phaidon); her first book, *Where They Create*, was published in 2011.

Pietje Tegenbosch is an art historian and art critic. She was a freelance contributor to Dutch newspapers *De Volkskrant* and *Het Parool*, and publishes in journals and catalogues. Tegenbosch was also connected with the AKZO Nobel Art Foundation, followed by working as advisor for the ABN AMRO Art Foundation. In that capacity, she was involved in establishing the Netherlands Association of Corporate Collections (Vereniging Bedrijfscollecties Nederland) of which she was a board member. She was chair of the jury of the Netherlands Royal Prize for Painting (Koninklijke Prijs voor Schilderkunst). Tegenbosch is a lecturer in art theory at the AKV St. Joost in Den Bosch. Since 2009, Tegenbosch and her partner Martin van Vreden have run gallery tegenboschvanvreden in Amsterdam, where, in addition to a program of international, contemporary art, she also organises a program of activities including lectures, performances, artist talks and screenings.

Colophon

This publication is published on the occasion of the exhibition 'Marcel Wanders: Pinned Up at the Stedelijk. 25 Years of Design', Stedelijk Museum Amsterdam, February 1 – June 15, 2014

Concept and compilation: Ingeborg de Roode
Editors: Ingeborg de Roode, Sophie Tates
Copy-editors: Stephanie Harmon, Dutton Hauhart
Texts: Marjan Groot, Jennifer Hudson, Alexandra Onderwater, Penny Sparke, Ingeborg de Roode, Pietje Tegenbosch, Robert Thiemann
Translation: Lisa Holden (D-EN)
Project management: Sophie Tates
Project assistant publications: Menno Dudok van Heel
Research support: Margreeth Soeting
Graphic design: Frame Publishers (Barbara Iwanicka and Cathelijn Kruunenberg)
Print: Poland
Publishers: Stedelijk Museum Amsterdam and Frame Publishers

With thanks to:
Anna Alberdingk Thijm, Jara Apeldoorn, Sarah de Boer-Schultz, Lucas Bonekamp, Elvie Casteleijn, Roos Hollander, Koos de Jong, Margriet Schavemaker, Jeroen Sondervan, Sasha Naod, Maarten Ternede, Valentina Zanobelli

Photo credits:
Artifort: 15
Alessi: 28
Marc Alt: 44
Droog Design: 17, 70
Cappellini: 28
Alberto Ferrero: 43, 106, 107
Fondation Le Corbusier: 41
Flos: 20, 36, 86
Goods: 111
Rene Gonkel: 172
Maarten van Houten, 37, 90, 91
Robbie Kavanagh: 74
Kvadrat: 23
Richard Learoyd: 71
Marsel Loermans: 72, 73
André Lichtenberg: 115
Peer Lindgreen: 35
Mandarina Duck: 108
Moooi: 21
Museum voor Moderne Kunst, Arnhem: 15
Daniël Nicolas: 174
Erwin Olaf & Marcel Wanders for Moooi 22, 29, 30, 35, 67-69, 113, 132, 145, 155
Inga Powilleit: 51, 52, 53, 107, 110, 176-177
Deidi von Schaewen: 49 (above)
Studio Bořek Šipek: 13

Stedelijk Museum Amsterdam: 13- 15, 18, 26, 125 (left), 162
Peter Tahl: 49 (below)
George Terberg: 43
Roberta Tinelli: 63, 94-95
Marcel Wanders Studio: 15, 16, 18, 20, 21, 24- 28, 30, 33, 34, 36, 37, 41, 42, 43-48, 54, 57, 59-63, 66, 71-85, 87-90, 92-107, 109-117, 119, 120, 122-131, 133-161, 163-175, 178-181, 190-192

The copyright from visual artists managed by a CISAC-organisation is held by Pictoright in Amsterdam © 2014, c/o Pictoright Amsterdam

© 2014 Stedelijk Museum Amsterdam, the authors and Frame Publishers Amsterdam. All rights reserved. No part of this publication may be reproduced, stored in a retrieval system, or transmitted in any form or by any means, electronic, mechanical, photocopying, recording or otherwise, without the prior written permission of the publisher. Although every effort was made to find the copyright holders for the illustrations used, it has not been possible to trace them all. interested parties are requested to contact Frame Publishers Amsterdam.

ISBN: 978-94-9172-728-3

Stedelijk Museum Amsterdam cat. no. 909

Cover design: based on Kameha Grand Bonn Hotel signature graphic and photograph for 'Pinned Up' project, designed by Marcel Wanders

Trade distribution USA and Canada:
Consortium Book Sales & Distribution, LLC.
34 Thirteenth Avenue NE, Suite 101
Minneapolis, MN 55413-1007
T +1 612 746 2600
T +1 800 283 3572 (orders)
F +1 612 746 2606

Distribution rest of world: Frame Publisher
www.frameweb.com
distribution@frameweb.com

Exhibition sponsor:

Main sponsor:

Partner: